Praise for my Best Shot

"No one has done so much to protect, and where necessary to restore, Montana's great fish and game populations and the habitats that sustain them as Jim Posewitz. This is his beautifully told, and sometimes gripping, story of why and how he did it. The plain fact is that "Poz" has been the mighty voice of the Montana conservation movement since the 1950s, and everybody who lives in this part of the country is in his debt."

—GORDON BRITTAN, REGENTS PROFESSOR OF PHILOSOPHY, MONTANA STATE UNIVERSITY-BOZEMAN

Conservation is never easy, never comfortable, and often inconvenient. A read of Jim Posewitz's life and career will inspire all of us that our work on behalf of landscapes and wild places will be our most rewarding endeavor, no matter how daunting the task or how slim the odds of success.

—RANDY NEWBERG, PUBLIC LAND HUNTER AND CREATOR OF FRESH TRACKS AND ON YOUR OWN ADVENTURES TELEVISION SHOWS

"Jim's latest book is the capstone on his body of work. Not only do you read Jim's path to his conservation ethic but you also learn how actions by individuals matter. Inspiring and a must read for the next generation of conservation soldiers!"

—LAND TAWNEY, 5TH GENERATION MONTANAN AND PRESIDENT & CEO OF BACKCOUNTRY HUNTERS & ANGLERS

"This book details an era in Montana when resource protection based on environmental legislation and individual activism reached its zenith. It is a case study of what an individual—Jim Posewitz—with some help from others, can accomplish given vision, foresight, drive, determination, and, at times, self-sacrifice. It is a story that needed to be told of an era and of a life well lived!"

—BOB MARTINKA, RETIRED AFTER A 30-YEAR CAREER WITH THE MONTANA DEPARTMENT OF FISH, WILDLIFE AND PARKS

MY Best Shot

Discovering and Living the Montana Conservation Ethic

Jim Posewitz

RIVERBEND
PUBLISHING

My Best Shot: Discovering and Living the Montana Conservation Ethic
Copyright © 2018 by Jim Posewitz

Published by Riverbend Publishing, Helena, Montana

ISBN 13: 978-1-60639-105-1

Printed in the United States of America.

1 2 3 4 5 6 7 8 9 0 VP 22 21 20 19 18

Cover and text design by Laurie "gigette" McGrath

Riverbend Publishing
P.O. Box 5833
Helena, MT 59604
1-866-787-2363
www.riverbendpublishing.com

Dedication

This work is dedicated to the field biologists who worked in the Ecological Services and Environment and Information Division of Montana Fish, Wildlife and Parks from 1969 through June of 1983. Their work ranged from wrestling grizzly bears and mountain goats in Montana's wildest places to escorting public information disseminators from New York's Madison Avenue down the longest free-flowing river in the lower forty-eight states. Their in-the-field efforts documented, revealed, and disseminated a new reality of what made ecosystems function and what it would take to preserve them. The political and bureaucratic struggles—where we took our best shots—were addressed with a vigor that could only come from knowing we carried the truth.

This work is also dedicated to the Montana citizens who have before and since our time in the sun stood up in defense of fish, wildlife, and the environment. They were doing it before Colonel Custer died in the Battle of the Little Bighorn and continue to do so well after we sent men to the moon and brought them back. This defense of nature and life on this planet was born in perhaps the only place it could happen—America's "New World" democracy, a place like no other where individuals can and have stood up to protect our unique *democracy of the wild*.

Also by Jim Posewitz

Beyond Fair Chase: The Ethic and Tradition of Hunting

*Inherit the Hunt: A Journey into the Heart of
American Hunting*

Rifle in Hand: How Wild America Was Saved

Taking a Bullet for Conservation

Acknowledgements

Thanks to wildlife conservation advocate and my wife Gayle Joslin for consistent and persistent review of this work as it developed. She also kept the freezer stocked with antelope, elk, and deer as I became preoccupied with this effort. Thanks also to Chris Cauble of Riverbend Publishing for suggesting this effort, editing the manuscript, and bringing the work to publication. Thanks are also extended to my friend, Laurie "Gigette" McGrath for her design help on all my many projects and books over the years.

Critical review on segments of this story were provided by my son Andrew, Robin Tawney Nichols, Bob Martinka, Larry Peterman, John Bailey, Steve Bayless, Bruce Rhewinkle, Ron Marcoux, Ralph Boland, and Jim Flynn. In all cases they sharpened my memory and in most cases they encouraged the telling of this story.

While all of these people provided valuable assistance, the author retains full responsibility for the concepts and details expressed in the telling of this story.

Contents

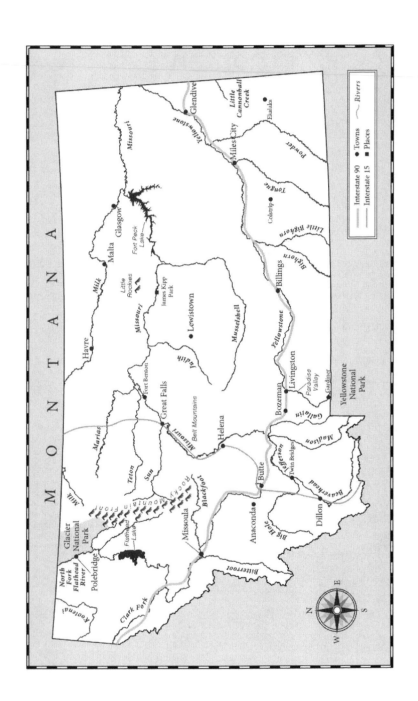

Introduction

Man's heart away from nature, becomes hard;
(the Lakota) knew that lack of respect for growing, living
things soon led to lack of respect for humans too.[1]

CHIEF LUTHER STANDING BEAR

"We have seen the 'dunya' and...it doesn't amount to anything." What came next was "ecstatic obliteration." It took the form of a gut-wrenching thud, a blinding flash, and a black smoky cloud of debris-filled dust packed with metal fragments and human body parts. The statement was that of a suicide bomber from occupied Gaza. It was his "final testament," a thought for us to contemplate as we struggle with the "why?" of it all. The word *"dunya"* means "physical world." In the bomber's judgment, the physical world he knew did not amount to anything, zero! And so he went angrily and eagerly to the hereafter of his faith.

I found the passage while reading a review of a book on suicide bombers. The line, haunting in its simplicity, still churns in my mind, returning time after time. When I watch the evening news from that troubled portion of our planet, my eyes are drawn past the smoldering wreckage and the wailing mourners to the *dunya* beyond. Now, for me, it is the image behind the headline that is the soul of each story. The image is of a landscape so lacking nourishment for the human spirit that suicide becomes casual, and leaving this physical world causes not a flicker of remorse.

[1] Taken from *Last Child in the Woods*, Richard Louv, Algonquin Books, 2008.

1

How different it is here in Montana. I love the physical world of my experience, wishing my own hereafter to be a familiar place, perhaps a *dunya* just like Montana where I have now spent most of my life. As our state slogan boasts, it is a "Last Best Place" at least deserving a niche in the great hereafter. And since there is still some doubt about the nature of the beyond that awaits us, I am in no hurry to leave this place. Montana has been my home for more than a half-century and because it amounts to something, it will most likely be what I see on my final day.

My coming to Montana bordered on accidental. In the middle of the 20th century, Montana State College in Bozeman decided they had had enough of losing and needed to field a competitive football team. Their recruiters cast a net that covered the mill and factory towns of the American heartland. Caught in that net, I became part of Montana State College's "Bobcat" team. It was the era of 60-minute football when everyone played both offense and defense. We met our arch rival University of Montana "Grizzlies" that first year with a lineup that was more than half freshmen, including me. It was my first start and the Grizzlies kicked our butts. When my teammates and I were seniors, we kicked theirs on the way to going undefeated and winning a national championship. The Montana State College Bobcats had become competitive, that contract fulfilled. It would not be long before the "College" became Montana State University with a very competitive academic and athletic environment.

When the 1956 Bobcats beat the Grizzlies in Missoula that year, it was the first time they had won there since 1902.[2] At that time, Theodore Roosevelt was the nation's president.

[2] Tom Donovan. *Montana's Greatest Rivalry: A College Football Classic.* Portage Meadows Publishing, Great Falls, Montana, 2014.

Bobcats 1956 Championship team (Jim Posewitz, number 85, front row)

Other memories of the college years had to do with more important things, like shooting my first deer. In January 1954 I borrowed a rifle, bought some shells, and shot a beautiful mule deer doe on the south end of the Bridger Mountains, about 300 yards north of the big white "M" on the mountainside. Dragging lunker brown trout out of the Madison River where it emerged from Bear Trap Canyon also rushes quickly to mind, the trout caught by dredging "sculpins." When the late fall storms were just right, bright-green-headed mallard ducks flocked to the spring creeks of the Gallatin Valley northwest of town and offered some fine shooting. The best hunts, however, came during the extended deer and elk hunting seasons of December and January. Football was finished, making it possible to concentrate on big mule deer bucks moving onto winter ranges and on elk leaving Yellowstone National Park.

My college transcript indicates there were classes, but they left little impression. One thing, however, does come clearly to mind. At the time, my fellow students and I never gave a moment's thought as to how those wonderful outdoor opportunities we savored had come to our time. We were never taught why those Bridger Mountains were public land, why that deer was there, or why I could be the hunter. We lived with the assumption that the Montana many of us had just met was simply always just like we found it. It took a long time for me to learn that Montana and its outdoor opportunities were not simply an accident in time and geography, waiting for me to show up. It was not a place so remote that it was spared the plunder and damage of a culture and a nation that set out to conquer and subdue the frontier. Like every other place in our nation, the natural resources, particularly the fish, wildlife, and wild land resources of Montana, went through a dark time when all might have been lost.

The wild abundance I found in the middle of the 20th century, and that we now see at the beginning of the 21st, is the result of more than a century of persistent and purposeful work. It was forged with a conservation ethic held by scores of Montanans and a handful of transients whose boots touched the Montana landscape. They were and still are a community of people that emerge from each succeeding generation who carry a powerful and persistent land ethic. And that is what brings us to the purpose of this writing. It is important that we recognize and appreciate their work and realize it is an effort that will always be a work in progress. The conservation ethic of generations of Montana people is the reason our dunya, our physical world, has a Bob Marshall Wilderness. It is the reason there is a free-flowing Yellowstone River, a Missouri River Breaks National Monument, a trout-laden Madison River, a Wild and Scenic Flathead River system, and thousands of "best places" large and small. When all these pieces began to fall together, Montana was judged to be the "Last Best Place." It was neither a false judgment nor an accident.

The people who carried this remarkable Montana conservation ethic came from all levels of society, ranging from pioneer miners and ranchers to a transient hunter who became the 26th President of the United States. Mostly, however, they were ordinary people who stepped up to do extraordinary things at the local level. They were civic organizations and rod-and-gun clubs banding together to tackle broader problems, and they were voters casting ballots reflecting the conservation ethic alive within the majority. Knowing some of the events and people that made the Montana we inherited happen will help us appreciate the effort that restored fish and wildlife to our time. Perhaps this awareness will motivate us to share the abundance that we enjoy, accept a responsibility to carry that ethic forward, and afford those who will follow us...wild places to be young in.

In October 2005, Montana newspapers carried a story under the headline "The Last Marine."[3] It was a story from the war in Iraq, a land that was once covered with a "forest so dense that the sunlight could not reach the ground."[4] The story was about the sole surviving Marine of a twelve-member squad of America's finest. This "last Marine" was from my town, had gone to the same high school as my sons, had played football and hockey and enjoyed great outdoor places. The story carried the following passage: "A Marine for three years [he] has decided not to re-enlist. Instead he thinks of home and fishing in the clear streams of Montana."

---

[3] "The Last Marine." Great Falls Tribune, No 143-121st Year, Great Falls, Montana, October 3, 2005.
[4] John Perlin. A Forest Journey. W.W. Norton & Company, New York – London, 1989.

5

Those "clear streams" are the physical world that this young man fought for, a place worth living for. Perhaps just the thought of them helped sustain him through a hellish experience. "The Last Marine" deserves no less than the "Last Best Place."

Finally, it is in large part a story of my time associated with Montana's wildness. This place has given so much beyond both my imagination and my expectation and I can only hope that my life here will have been a positive thing. The stories that follow are told from the perspective of an 18-year-old who wandered into Montana and had quite a ride!

Setting the Stage

There is a period in American history remembered as the "Dirty Thirties." That period was dominated by "The Great Economic Depression," the "Drought," and the "Dust Bowl." Author Timothy Egan describes it in great detail in his book *The Worst Hard Times*. My mind tends to focus on a day in the middle of that dirty decade and on an event that Egan describes in its dark and stark reality:

> A Sunday in Mid-April 1935....The air crackled with electricity. Snap. Snap. Snap. Birds screeched and dashed for cover. As the black wall approached, car radios clicked off, overwhelmed by the static. Ignitions shorted out. Waves of sand, like ocean water rising over a ship's prow, swept over roads. Cars went into ditches. A train derailed....That was Black Sunday, April 14, 1935, day of the worst duster of them all... More than 300,000 tons of Great Plains topsoil was airborne that day.

I was one month plus eight days old when that duster blew off the Great Plains on its way to the Atlantic Ocean. Living on the west shore of Lake Michigan, my first taste of the American West occurred on that day when I sucked in that dirty air as I wailed for a clean set of drawers.

When I was one-year-old, Franklin Delano Roosevelt called for the first North American Wildlife Conference to breathe new life into the American conservation reformation

7

launched four decades earlier by his fifth cousin, Theodore Roosevelt. These were events in our great American democracy around which my entire life would be molded. Thus, before tracking this portion of my life's journey, there is a need to take a look at a bit of our nation's history. When a person decides to get on this conservation train, either as a professional manager or citizen advocate, it is well to realize that it is in all ways a train in motion and to appreciate where it has been.

This great nation of ours was founded on an exceptional set of basic human rights holding that all men were created free and equal before God and each other. The founding documents— the Declaration of Independence, the Constitution, and the Bill of Rights—addressed those human issues. There was no reference to fish or wildlife, nor did any of those documents suggest a conservation ethic. We were a nation of people free to find our own way. We indeed stumbled forward.

Following the Louisiana Purchase, the French took an interest in the development of the American democracy. A generation later, a French nobleman, Alexis de Tocqueville, visited America in the 1830s and wrote about what he saw in *Democracy in America,* published in 1835. He observed:

> I confess that in America I saw more than America; I sought the image of democracy itself, with its inclinations, its character, its prejudices, and its passions, in order to learn what we have to fear or hope from its progress.

In addition, de Tocqueville apparently found the idea of conservation to be totally lacking in our fledgling nation:

In Europe people talk a great deal of the wilds of America, but the Americans themselves never think about them; they are insensible to the wonders of inanimate nature. Their eyes are fired with another sight; they march across these wilds, clearing swamps, turning the courses of rivers....[5]

At another point he observed:

[The American people] may be said not to perceive the mighty forests that surround them till they fall beneath the hatchet.[6]

Perhaps the nobleman de Tocqueville perceived a flaw in the democratic notions fueling the engines of the young nation recently born of revolution.

Sixty-six years after America declared its independence, and eight years after de Tocqueville's writings, the new country's Supreme Court made a huge decisions that opened a path on which a conservation ethic might emerge. The court ruled that by virtue of the Declaration of Independence, the people in America had declared themselves "sovereign." The court further noted that, in that capacity, the rights and privileges formerly held by the English Crown (the previous sovereign) had passed to the states to be managed as a public trust for the good of the people. In other words, the "king's deer" of "Old Europe" had become the *people's deer* in this "New World" democracy. This important determination established a legal cornerstone that would have a significant impact on America

[5] Peter Wild, *Pioneer Conservationists of Eastern America.* Mountain West Publishing Company, Missoula, Montana, 1986.
[6] Alexis de Tocqueville. 1832. From: *A Nation's Natural Resource Legacy.* USDA Forest Service, April 1999. FS-630.

and ultimately the world. In time, subsequent decisions also supported the public ownership and public-trust management of fish and wildlife.

At the time there was little indication that America would find a conservation ethic big enough to create an American commons out of which would emerge national forests, a wilderness system, parks, national monuments, wildlife refuges, game ranges, a wild and scenic river system, hunting and fishing for every American with the desire to do so, and a fish and wildlife resource capable of sustaining it all. Still, in time, all those things would happen and Montana played an important role in the happening.

Naturalists Ralph Waldo Emerson, Henry David Thoreau, and George Perkins Marsh all thought, wrote, lectured, and died before Theodore Roosevelt shot one of the last wild, free-ranging buffalo on Little Cannonball Creek, Montana Territory, in 1883. It was a seminal moment in American history that would soon lead to a conservation epiphany and ultimately a conservation ethic that built a stage on which that baby born on the shore of Lake Michigan in the middle of the "Dirty Thirties" could play out a wonderful life.

Finding Montana

I came awake well before first light. The soothing rhythm of iron wheels clicking and clacking across the gaps between the steel rails was not enough to secure what might have been an easy slumber. It was August 1953. I was in my eighteenth year and about to see the American West for the first time.

My mom and dad had driven us from our home in Sheboygan, Wisconsin, to the railroad hub in Minneapolis to put me on the train to Bozeman. Some years later my mom told me of that moment. The waiting room of the depot was separated from the boarding platform by swinging doors with glass windows. As she watched me walk out down a flight of stairs and disappear into one of the train's passenger cars, she took note of the fact that I never looked back or turned to wave goodbye. While I now realize what that did to her, I still wonder about what that said about me.

In time, I learned that a routine medical check-up as an infant revealed that I had a heart murmur that could not be explained. My tearful mother was said to have taken a bucket and brush and scrubbed the concrete steps leading to our parish church in support of her prayers that I'd be given a normal life. In my 75th year I learned that I had been born with a bicuspid aortic valve rather than the normal tricuspid valve. It was a malady that remained undiscovered until, after a rather strenuous life in the Northern Rockies, I was in the middle of my eighth decade. Statistics suggested I should have been dead before the end of my fifth decade. My mom knew how to talk to the Lord. I should have turned to wave.

The sun had finished with the day somewhere between

my boarding the train in Minneapolis and the North Dakota border. The dark hours that followed were interrupted only by dimly lit depot platforms of small towns and hamlets scattered across a great expanse of darkness. One of those hamlets must have been Medora, North Dakota, but it would be a very long time before I would learn of events that centered around that place and how they affected just about everything I would do and come to value.

After a short stop in Glendive, Montana, to exchange passengers, freight, and the U.S. mail, we slipped again into the prairie night. Before the next stop, first light raised the curtain on what was about to become my home. Dawn revealed we were following the Yellowstone River westward. A quarter century later, Montana extended an unprecedented mantel of protection over the waters of the Yellowstone and its tributaries. It was an action giving this longest free-flowing river in the Lower 48 states a chance to remain free flowing, and I would give seven years of my professional life, and a significant portion of my soul, to that effort. For the moment, I only wondered how soon I would see the mountains and what might be the name of that long-tailed black and white bird I had seen for the first time.

A good part of that first day in Montana was spent following the upstream grade along the Yellowstone. After Billings, the Beartooth Plateau and Absaroka Mountains came into view and dominated the southern horizon. As we approached Livingston, the Crazy Mountains appeared to the north. In time I would come to learn the names of these places, become intimate with their geography and with the politics of their protection. For now, curious and full of youthful energy, I was left to wonder what it would be like to approach their mass and perhaps challenge their summits. West of Livingston we hit the final grade, a slow climb over Bozeman Pass, and a cautious descent through a narrow canyon. For the first time I actually felt "in the mountains" of my expectations and imagination. Then, suddenly, it was into the open again, the Gallatin Valley—the end of my ticket.

With a suitcase in each hand I stood for a moment on the platform, breathed my lungs full of crisp pine-scented air, and entered the depot. I was clueless as to my next move, had no idea where the campus was or how to get there. Looking around, I spotted a rather stout young man that I judged to be slightly older than myself. I also judged that he just might be in Bozeman for the same purpose. Having few other choices, I approached him, introduced myself and my reason for being there, and simply hoped for a positive response. I had just met Robert Pewitt Jr., upperclassman, Montana State College "Bobcats" fullback, heavyweight wrestler, and cowboy from southern Phillips County in eastern Montana. I had also met a person who was very quiet, a bit shy, soft spoken, and caring with a heart as big as, well, Phillips County. Big Bob decided, probably right there on the spot, that he just found a stray calf that needed looking after, and he would provide it. It was the cowboy way.

Upon reaching the campus and the Bobcats' training camp, I quickly learned that the coach who had recruited me had forgotten my name; there were 100 players in camp and only 33 available scholarships; there were no junior varsity or freshman teams; those who suited up for the first game would get the scholarships; and we would practice three times a day. In high school I played tight end on offense and middle linebacker on defense. When the Bobcats' first "roster and depth chart" was posted, Sheboygan's all-conference middle linebacker found his name listed as the seventh-string left end. It was one of life's low points, but there was hope. Maybe the heart murmur would show up, the physical exam would be flunked, and I'd be sent home without dishonor. Simply quitting was not an option.

About a week into camp, the coach scheduled our first full-contact scrimmage. He had a pretty good idea of who he wanted for his first-string starters and he wanted to instill confidence in that unit. What better way to build confidence in a right-handed running team than to send them against a freshman seventh-string left defensive end? On that particular afternoon however, the offense could not pick up much yardage. At one point, amid his growing frustration, the head coach, who now remembered my name, "counseled" me to "*@#$%&! Posewitz, play that position right!*" But an assistant coach took me aside and suggested, "Just hang in there kid and keep knocking 'em down." I did.

During the pre-practice team meeting the next morning, the head coach apologized to me in front of the whole team, which was unprecedented in my experience, and I moved up on the roster. The 1952 Bobcats had won two games and lost eight. In 1953 we won four and lost four. Recovery was on its way.

When Thanksgiving came in 1953, none of the midwestern recruits had any place to go for the short holiday. Trains and buses were too slow and commercial air travel virtually non-existent. Team members from Montana filled the gap, and Bob Pewitt invited me to his home to meet a piece of Americana that I thought had vanished. It was the first of several trips to the Pewitt ranch at Thanksgiving and on spring break during my college years.

The Pewitt ranch was north of the Missouri River on the prairie just off an isolated mountain range called "The Little

Rockies." Since there were no bridges across the Missouri River between Fort Benton and Fort Peck Dam, and the ferryboats had all been pulled out for the winter, the trip from Bozeman to his home near Zortman was a long, circuitous ride.

Car-pooling with other students heading for communities along Montana's northern "Hi-Line," we traveled a course that was in many ways a preview of coming attractions. They were places that would enter, periodically re-enter, and ultimately fill my life. The route from Bozeman went west to Three Forks where the Missouri River is formed. From there it was north through Helena and into the Prickly Pear Canyon where ten years later I became engaged in the battle to prevent highways from altering stream channels. After that it was still on to the north through Great Falls and the granddaddy of all Montana towns, Fort Benton. In the 1960s I would return to Fort Benton to engage the U.S. Corps of Engineers in spirited debate over the fate of the Missouri River. The river, indifferent to our arguments, nevertheless was spared the indignity of being dammed at Cow Island and Fort Benton. It then became a "wild and scenic river" and ultimately entered the 21st century as a national monument. Our car of holiday-spirited students, interested in only the moment, continued north to Havre, then east to Malta where Bob and I were deposited at the Great Northern Hotel to await his parents.

The Great Northern Hotel was a classic Montana meeting place with wood and leather chairs arranged so patrons could look onto Malta's main street. About all I remember about the décor was an old photo of a freight team that was enlarged to the extent that it covered nearly one entire wall. It was a photo taken in 1907 of a multi-team hitch of horses hauling freight from the Missouri River to the gold mining towns of Zortman and Landusky in the Little Rockies. The freight outfit belonged to Joe Hartman, and I would meet Joe before the day was out. Joe was Bob's uncle and he lived with them on the ranch. The big mural, along with the original hotel, have since been reduced to ashes.

It wasn't long before Bob's dad and mom arrived and we began the last leg of our journey south from Malta into the darkness of southern Phillips County. There were no yard lights to compromise the night and no perceptible evidence of kerosene lamps that might have sent a glow against the window of one of the widely scattered ranch houses. Electricity had not yet found southern Phillips County. Beyond the headlights piercing the way ahead, the darkness was absolute. After about an hour we left the main road, wandered through a series of unmarked dirt roads, up a long single-lane and then, out of all that endless blackness, the headlights reflected off a low, single-story log structure, the Pewitt ranch house. We were home.

Before first light, Bob, lantern in hand, led me to a big frame barn, introduced me to the work team, and instructed me in the fine art of harnessing and hitching horses to a wagon. There was hay to be tossed. After all, it was late November and the college boys needed a little exercise. We also learned there were some yearling steers that needed branding, and that work would involve Bob's relatives on nearby ranches. While I don't recall much of the details, it was quite a gathering. One of the uncles would rope a yearling steer by a hind leg and then the cowboys would order the two "Bobcats" into the fray. One of us would grab the rope and the other the yearling's tail, topple the beast and then grab a front leg in a sort of hammerlock, thus holding the critter for branding. The cowboys had great fun commenting on our straightforward technique, and we were loving it!

The Pewitt Ranch, 1953 *(Photo by Jim Posewitz)*

The mid-day event on branding day made a mark on my memory that has not dimmed in more than a half-century. First was the lunch. We sat at a long makeshift table laden with food. Then the women marched in with platters piled high with T-bone steaks. In my mind's eye I can still see those sizzling beauties in front of me. The other impression was how vigorous all the men looked, and how worn all the women appeared. It was a hard way, their workload was staggering, it was without a single convenience, and it took a toll.

Sometime during that holiday period I had cause to go to the outhouse in the middle of the night. The night was moonless, clear, and November crisp. For the first few paces beyond the cabin door my eyes were fixed to the path. Then, rather slowly looking skyward, I beheld the cosmos wrapping itself around me from horizon to horizon in a massive dome of sparkling brilliance that literally drove me to my knees. It was undiluted, without smoke, smog, or one particle of particulate matter, and there was not a light bulb within 60 miles in any direction. As a youngster learning to camp in the Midwest I had seen stars before, usually through a hole in a canopy of trees. Now I had just witnessed the true expanse of the midnight heavens, and from that moment I knew I was home. Even now, try as I might, I cannot remember a single Thanksgiving holiday during the first seventeen years of my life, but I cannot and will not ever forget the eighteenth. It was the year I came home for the first time.

Professional Preparation

When leaving Wisconsin in August 1953, I made another big mistake in addition to not saying goodbye to my mother. I had promised my summer employer that I would return for another season's work. Thus I returned for another summer at Silver Moon Springs Trout Farm. The place was a commercial trout farm with fishing ponds. The customers paid for what they caught and while Silver Moon Springs was honest and educational work, much of the summer of 1954 was spent gutting trout by the bucket full. That fall, when time came to return to college, no promises were made.

The Summer of 1955

While the football season and the academic year established life's pattern and rhythm, it was the summer field seasons that provided the real education and most vivid memories. During the summer of 1955 the Tiber Dam was being constructed on the Marias River. The Montana Department of Fish and Game, under the leadership of their regional fisheries manager, Nels Thoreson, had taken on an enormous and probably unprecedented project. The objective was to purge non-native fish from the headwaters of the Marias down to the dam. The dam would form a barrier to upstream movement of carp and other "rough fish," so waters above the dam would once again be home to native fish. It was a monumental task and every available fisheries worker along with area game wardens were rallied to the task. We camped in an empty building at the Cut Bank airport. We were surrounded by sacks of "Fish-Tox," a poison designed to kill fish.

Being young and reasonably fit, another summer student field worker, Delano (Laney) Hanzel, and I were assigned to the "slough crew." We were each provided with a tin backpack used by firefighters to spray water on flames. Our packs were loaded with Fish-Tox blended with water. The fish-killing procedure was for the main crew to apply the poison to a stream and then have the "slough crew" follow the toxic water downstream on foot and spray any backwater or isolated puddle with the mixture in our backpack tanks. Much of the time was spent on tributaries flowing through the Blackfeet Indian Reservation.

During that summer, we found ourselves working Cut Bank Creek, Badger Creek, and the Two Medicine River, all headwater tributaries of the Marias. Whenever we encountered someone living on or near a stream, we would explain what we were doing and ask permission to work through their property. When we sought permission to walk through one particular place, the resident Native American responded: "First you take the buffalo, then you kill all the coyotes, and now you want to kill the fish! You are not coming through here!"

What I didn't know then, but came to appreciate later in life, was that the Marias River was named by the Lewis and Clark Expedition. I also learned that Captain Lewis had a violent conflict with a band of young Blackfeet on the Two Medicine River in July 1806. The result was two dead Blackfeet and Captain Lewis and associates in a full-gallop flight back to the Missouri River.[7] A century and forty-nine years separated these two events when a descendant of those warriors denied us access. While not appreciating

[7] Stephan E. Ambrose. *Undaunted Courage*. Touchstone, New York, NY, 1996.

the consistency just encountered, we respected the denial, and got off easy. We resumed our mission downstream from his property.

The other memorable event of that summer was cleaning the carp out of "Shit Creek." At the time, the city of Shelby had a community sewer system, but either a marginal treatment plant or none at all. Thus, a once dry coulee was carrying the city's effluent down into the Marias River. A casual inspection of this "tributary" revealed the presence of carp, one of the exotic fish we were trying to eliminate. In an unprecedented display of creativity, the fish-killing crew rented a couple of motel rooms in Shelby, purchased an adequate supply of beer, and began to party. The main entertainment was mixing Fish-Tox in the toilets and flushing the contents into the sewer system. We referred to the toilets as the "headwater springs of Shit Creek." We cannot say we cleaned up the creek, but we did kill the carp.

The Summer of 1956

During the summer of 1956, the United States Forest Service was spraying the national forests in Montana with DDT, the powerful (and now banned) insecticide. The objective was to kill the spruce bud worm, an insect that was damaging fir trees. The method of application was aerial spraying. Of course, DDT killed all insects, including those insects living in streams and feeding trout.

My assignment that summer was to lead an electro-fishing field crew to sample some of the streams that might be affected by the spraying. The streams monitored included Canyon Creek and Trapper Creek in the Deerlodge National Forest; Trout Creek, Beaver Creek and Crow Creek in the Helena National Forest; and Sheep Creek in the Lewis and

Clark National Forest. We sampled the streams prior to the application of DDT, immediately after application, and finally late in the summer. In addition, we put sheets of sensitive paper over or adjacent to the streams to record whether or not the spray drifted directly into the streams.

The Forest Service and the Montana Fish and Game Department were having a vigorous debate over the spraying. At the end of the summer, our data showed that the drifting spray indeed fell directly into streams; the condition of the fish was enhanced immediately after the spray as they consumed a mother lode of drifting dead insects; and there was a late summer fish mortality when all the bugs were gone and the fish relied on their own fat reserves, which were now laden with DDT. One day when electro-fishing Sheep Creek, we waded through a deep, still pool and were struck by a strange odor coming from the bottom of the pool. It turned out the pool had served as a kind of settling basin and our wading had stirred up the dead insects collected there. We were knee deep in a rotting mass of dead mayflies, caddis flies, and stoneflies.

The Summer of 1957

Dr. Claudius Jethro Daniels Brown was the fisheries professor at Montana State College. To us students he was more simply Dr. C. J. D. ("Kingfish") Brown. In addition to being a wonderful person and excellent instructor, he wrote a book entitled *Fishes of Montana*. Following graduation with a bachelor's degree in fish and wildlife management, I became eligible for the military draft under provisions of the Selective Service Act. While waiting for the draft board to call, I had a diploma and time on my hands. Dr. Brown was polishing up the manuscript for his book and hired me to see if there was any species of fish that had been overlooked.

Armed with just about every fish-collecting apparatus and specimen preservative available, stuffed into a Fish and Game Department suburban, a seasonal assistant and I took to the waters. For collecting the fish we packed an electro-fishing outfit, seines, gill nets, Fish-Tox, and that ultimate fish collector—dynamite. For preserving specimens we had jars of alcohol and cream cans slopping full of formaldehyde. Thus armed, we took off shocking, netting, poisoning and blasting fish from border to border.

We hit the road in June when most western Montana streams were high with runoff, so we headed east to find and sample streams that were part of the Belle Fourche and Little Missouri drainages. These were the tributaries in Montana that flowed into Wyoming, South Dakota, and North Dakota. Then we headed north to where the Poplar and Milk River drainages slipped into Montana from Canada on their way to the Missouri River. As the summer wore on, we focused on Glacier National Park's "triple divide" and the Saint Mary drainage flowing from Glacier into Canada's Hudson Bay and eventually the Arctic Ocean, but not before it sent some diverted water into the Milk River. Our grand finale was setting off eight sticks of dynamite in a rock-walled Kootenai River canyon in a vain attempt to add a white sturgeon to Dr. Brown's collection.

I spent the remainder of 1957 working a Fish and Game hunter check station and hunting. It all resulted in an antelope in the Judith Basin, a mountain goat in the Crazy Mountains, and a spike bull elk in the Gravelly Range. As the year neared its end, I received a letter from my draft board stating that "your friends and neighbors have selected you to serve."

In late November I found myself in a room full of draftees at Fort Leonard Wood in Missouri. A person of importance entered the room, stood behind a microphone and podium, and asked, "Is there anyone in this room with a college degree?" I was the only person in the room to stand up. His next question was, "What is your degree in soldier?" My response was, "Fish and wildlife management—sir!" Without the slightest moment of hesitation, he said, "Sit down."

Thus my military career was launched. It was brief but like every step in life, it carried lessons to be learned. After basic infantry training at Fort Leonard Wood, there was advanced infantry training at Fort Benning, Georgia. In May 1958, as part of the 3rd Infantry Division, we shipped to Germany. On my last furlough before shipping over, I married my college sweetheart, Helen Vidal. She came to Germany independently and found a little apartment in charming Bamberg within walking distance of the military compound.

Military life was as good as could be hoped for. My time was served after the fighting stopped in Korea and before it began in Viet Nam. Although the "Iron Curtain" divided Europe, the damage of World War II was receding. To fill the time, the military organized a U.S. Army Europe football conference. I played tight end for the Bamberg Riders and we won the European championship. Playing football was classified as "temporary duty" or in military jargon, "TDY." The coach's pep talk before each game was the same, "do or die for TDY." It was good duty. In addition to military business and football, I joined the base's rod and gun club and began studying the German hunting system and traditions. My objective was to become a qualified hunter in Germany and then be invited on a hunt, but my tour of duty was too short to make this happen. Military "leave" or vacation time did gives us the opportunity to briefly tour France, England,

Switzerland, Austria, and southern Germany, including the "October Fest" in Munich.

Immediately following an honorable discharge it was back to Bozeman for graduate school. Two days after exiting the military, the family grew by one with the birth of our first son, Eric. Graduate school was financed by serving as a graduate assistant football coach, Helen's work as a medical technologist, and my seasonal work with the Fish and Game Department. In nineteen months, with a Master of Science Degree in Fish and Wildlife Management, it was time to go to work. The family, now including sons Eric and Brian, headed for Great Falls. My first permanent job was as a fisheries biologist for the Montana Fish and Game Department.

A Career is Launched

Somewhere around April Fool's Day of 1961, my 32-year career with the Montana Fish and Game Department began. Since there were no college offerings that touched on Montana's conservation history, the extent and potential of that knowledge would not be appreciated until discovered many decades later. Although we were taught the fundamentals of fish and wildlife biology, the social and cultural forces that brought those resources to my generation and custody remained a complete blank. Had my starting date been a mere three years later it would have coincided with the 100th anniversary of the first Montana legislation to protect fish. I was near retirement before that fact was learned.

What I would eventually learn was that Montana Territorial Legislators began protecting fish in 1864, during their very first assembly. The heroes of Montana's seminal fish and wildlife conservation ethic were the brothers James and Granville Stuart. In 1857 the Stuarts rode into Montana over what would become Monida Pass. They were young gold miners and adventurers trying to get back to Iowa after trying their luck on the California gold fields. The Mormon War blocked the eastern road from Salt Lake City, so the Stuarts detoured north and found the natural wonders of Montana to their liking. On the 4th of July, 1863, these pioneer miners, ranchers, statesmen, and conservationists celebrated the nation's birthday with a dinner of fish caught from the Clark Fork River. Granville's diary noted: "July 4, 1863, James and Clabber, our Indian horse herder, caught twenty-five large trout and we celebrated the national day by having a fine dinner with trout as the principal dish." Two days later he would note: "July 6, 1863 I caught thirty-five trout using grasshoppers for bait."

A year later Montana became a Territory, and Granville wrote:

> The Deer Lodge Valley is famous for two things, one is that mountain trout are more plenty in it than any other place of the same extent in the world… if the legislature does not enact some laws in regard to game and fish, there will not be in a few years so much as a minnow or deer left alive in all the territory.[8]

As delegates to the first and subsequent Montana Territorial Legislatures, the Stuarts introduced and saw to passage, laws that expressed a conservation ethic held by at least some, perhaps many, pioneers. The first legislation was introduced by James; it restricted the taking of fish to a hook and line, thus ending the commercial seining of trout for local markets. That 1864 law also had the effect of prohibiting the dynamiting of fish. That was an exceptional preemptive move since it would be another three years before that particular compound was invented and patented. In a territory soon to be settled by droves of hungry miners, that legislation turned out to be more than visionary. In 1872, Granville Stuart introduced and was able to pass legislation that sought to protect buffalo and other wildlife with designated hunting seasons. To put this frontier commitment to a fish and wildlife conservation ethic in some perspective, these actions were taken years before Colonel Custer and the troopers of

---

[8] Joan Louise Brownell. *The Genesis of Wildlife Conservation in Montana*. Master's Thesis, Montana State University. Bozeman, Montana. 1987.

the 7th U.S. Cavalry met their demise on the hills above the Little Bighorn River in 1876.

Granted, at the time there was no infrastructure to enforce fish and game laws. However, what is most important is that the Stuarts recognized and represented the value of the publicly owned fish and wildlife resources. I was about to take my first steps along a career path to do that very same thing, but at the time I knew nothing about these early pioneers who blazed the trail that I would put my feet to nearly a century later.

My very first project as a full-time employee of the Montana Fish and Game Department was retrieving gill nets that a crew had abandoned the fall before when the reservoir they were sampling froze over before they could remove the nets. The local game warden called in with word that the ice had gone out and the nets had blown ashore. I spent the next day and a half removing rotting fish, mostly suckers, out of the gill nets and then learning how to mend salvaged nets. Thus a career in science-based fish and wildlife resource management was launched.

As it turned out, the early 1960s were very important years in the evolution of natural resource management in the Montana Fish and Game Department. This was particularly true in the Fisheries Division. The federal Dingle-Johnson Act that taxed fishing equipment and made that source of revenue available for fish restoration and management was relatively new. The act was passed in the 1950s, and state agencies responded by hiring biologists trained to work on problems affecting that resource. Prior to this federal focus and stimulus, fisheries work was generally centered on setting seasons and creel limits, and raising hatchery fish for stocking. That was about to change.

The Fish Needed a Plan

In the early 1960s, one thing that a good number of fisheries managers and researchers had in common was a fondness for beer. Thus, during the annual meetings of the Fisheries Division biologists, it was not surprising to find many of them assembled every evening in the bar of the motel or hotel where the meeting was held. In the spring of 1961, such a gathering occurred well after the normal meetings of the day. The senior members of the group were seated around a table with us junior new arrivals more or less standing behind them. The topic, as always, quickly went to what was learned in the fish population studies under way.

On that particular evening, a consensus was expressed that preserving Montana's trout stream fisheries was not really reliant on setting fishing seasons, or imposing creel limits, or distributing hatchery produced trout. The issue demanding attention was preserving and perhaps restoring trout habitat so they just might be able to take care of themselves. Those assembled already knew: bulldozing stream channels into straight-line ditches clobbered fish populations; depleted water flows left channels parched and barren of fish; and that the Clark Fork River from Butte to Missoula had been a toxic tomb for fish for a century because of mining pollution. One of the division's elders grabbed a handy bar napkin and recorded the future course just agreed upon by the assembled.

The plan was as beautiful in its simplicity as it was powerful in its logic and, ultimately, in its impact. There were no "planning facilitators" or rooms decorated with sheets of "flow charts" and recorded "inputs." There was only one tiny bar napkin on which was written: "preserve the physical channel; clean up the polluted waters; and, give fish a water right."

At the time there was no prohibition to anyone bulldozing streams; the water quality laws were marginal at best; and to claim water for any "beneficial use," it had to be taken out of the streambed. While the fate of that napkin isn't known, the direction it charted was locked into the minds and mission of those assembled. Although it would be a rough and rocky ride, in less than two decades those three goals would all be achieved.

The final act of those assembled in that Billings hotel bar was to set priorities for the three major goals. It was quickly agreed by consensus that protecting the physical channel was the top priority because once the channel was gone, the effects of addressing water quality and quantity would be limited. But if the channel was preserved, then improvements in water quality and in-stream flow rights for fish could be achieved in the future. At that point the bar management began blinking the lights off and on, a traditional signal that it was closing time, and the ground-breaking fisheries meeting was thus adjourned.

Taking the First Step for Stream Channel Preservation

While the fisheries biologists were taking aim at stream channel preservation, construction of the interstate highways in Montana was just getting under way. One of the first segments under construction was through Little Prickly Pear Canyon between Helena and Great Falls. The narrow canyon already had a trout stream, a two-lane highway, and a railroad stuffed into it. Laying a four-lane interstate on top of all that left little room for negotiation. Efforts to relocate the interstate to an alternative route, bypassing the canyon, were dead on arrival. In addition, highway engineers were dedicated to building highways in the most cost-efficient manner, meaning as straight as possible and as few bridges as possible.

Our time in the field on this project was measuring the damage and making it the "poster child" for needing a law to protect stream channels. It was reasoned that most state legislators from northern and eastern Montana would travel through that canyon on their way to the 1963 legislative session. They would be forced to travel on an interstate highway under construction. We decided they needed to know that a treasured Montana trout stream was trying to meander beneath all the rubble and debris.

The big break in the legislative campaign came when the Montana Junior Chamber of Commerce decided that preserving trout streams was a good idea, and that stream channel protection was a good place to start. Behind the internal leadership of Harry B. Mitchell a young Great Falls dairyman, they dedicated themselves to achieving the appropriate legislation to help make that happen. At the same time, the Montana Fish and Game Department put together a public information program relative to the damage that channelizing trout streams did to fish populations. That effort involved their public information officers and fish biologists taking to the streets with colored slide shows and lectures, appearing before anybody who would listen. The result was the first stream channel preservation act in the nation. As amended and finally passed in 1963, the "Montana Stream Protection Act" affected only divisions of the state government. It required any component of state government to notify the Fish and Game Department of any plans to change a stream channel. If Fish and Game did not approve, it would have to offer an alternative to what was proposed. With this law, protection of fish habitat had just broken a legal barrier and gained legitimate representation. Nonetheless, there was considerable concern that Fish and Game would stop all highway construction, so the 1963 act was written to expire in two years. It would be up to the next Legislature to renew it—or not. Thus, Fish and Game had to demonstrate they could make this law work or they would lose it.

Big Waters, Big Lessons

The Yellowstone and Missouri Rivers

While the Fish and Game Department began a focused administration of the Stream Preservation Act, I was offered a chance to become the regional fisheries manager in northeast Montana. Although I did not have enough tenure to qualify for the position, I accepted and moved out to Glasgow in September 1962. Before we left, we spent Labor Day camped in Glacier National Park with friends Lou and Linda Wendt. Lou had introduced me to rock climbing while we were both in graduate school. On this trip he led me up the north face of Chief Mountain while the ladies and youngsters spent the day at the mountain's base camp. It would be decades before I learned that Chief Mountain was sacred to Native Americans. Since becoming aware of that fact, I continue to thank the mountain for indulging my stumbling transgression.

Within a few days we were headed east across the northern plains. At the time, considerable fisheries work had been done on the management of farm ponds and the various fish species that might survive in eastern Montana and create recreational fisheries. It was with that expectation that I packed up my family and belongings and headed to Glasgow to see what could be learned and done. The growing family now included sons Eric, Brian, and Allen.

As it turned out, the "farm pond" needing attention was the quarter-million-acre Fort Peck Reservoir along with the wild, 180-mile tributary that fed it, the Missouri River. Our fisheries science, technology, and equipment was more than a bit inadequate for those tasks. Stream electrofishing technology of the day was still restricted to streams that could be waded and blocked with nets. The gear available for sampling standing water was available, but the size of this "pond" was indeed intimidating. There is only so far that a person can row in a day, and if that day turns out to be windy, the challenge was daunting. The fisheries crew for the region was me, and on occasion, one or two summer field workers. The seasonal help was often one university fisheries student and one local schoolteacher on summer break.

To round out the challenge, I was informed that a mysterious run of paddlefish was showing up in the lower Yellowstone River, also a part of my region of responsibility. The fish were relatively small for paddlefish, all very uniform in size, and they were being snagged by fishermen below an irrigation diversion. A trip to Glendive was clearly in order, and we were confident the data we needed to get started would be available in a placed named "The Beer Jug."

As it turned out, most of the above fishery management challenges were solving themselves while we stood on shoreline or riverbank wondering where to start. The U.S. Army Corps of Engineers had recently finished construction of Garrison Dam on the Missouri River in North Dakota, just below where the Yellowstone River merged with the Missouri. Anxious to fill Garrison Reservoir, water managers had released more water from Fort Peck Reservoir, greatly lowering its water level, a condition that would persist for years. Terrestrial vegetation rapidly reclaimed the reservoir's exposed shoreline and mud flats. On the North Dakota side, the inundation of fertile river bottom along with adjacent grasslands and farms produced what was initially a well fertilized, nutrient rich, relatively fish-barren environment available for nature to fill.

As we pieced together the filling of Garrison Reservoir,

along with the experience of The Beer Jug patrons we interviewed, it appeared there was an exceptional population of young paddlefish coming up the Yellowstone River. Native paddlefish were present in the Missouri and Yellowstone rivers, and we surmised that the nutrient rich waters of the new lake facilitated the growth of plankton and algae, which benefited the survival of young paddlefish. The paddlefish being taken at that moment in history, in addition to their uniformity is size, were almost exclusively male fish. The fact that male paddlefish mature about four years earlier than females solved the mystery of size uniformity and the gender dominance at that moment in the fishery.

Fort Peck Reservoir water levels were gradually restored. As they were, the terrestrial vegetation that had grown on the exposed mud flats and shoreline provided excellent spawning and rearing habitat for yellow perch, black crappies, and northern pike. Since there had been many hundreds of miles of exposed shoreline, the result was quite dramatic and the few anglers who were there were happy. So two of the Glasgow Region's major fish management mysteries pretty much solved themselves. We eagerly awaited a new challenge.

It was not a long wait. Now that Garrison Reservoir was completed, it was probably imperative that the dam builders find their next project. The Corps of Engineers turned their attention to the last piece of the Missouri River that remained undammed. The agency produced a comprehensive plan offering a number of alternatives for the river from Fort Peck to the base of Morony Dam at Great Falls.

At the time there were no environmental protection laws at either the national or state level. There was, at the federal level, a Fish and Wildlife Coordination Act that required federal agencies to communicate with the U.S. Fish and Wildlife Service relative to what they would recommend to minimize damage to fish and wildlife, but there was no requirement that those recommendations be followed. The only barrier the dam builders had to get over was securing an appropriation of funds from Congress, and that only required some political pressure to make it happen.

The river segments to be dammed in Montana were the last remnants of what was once the mighty Missouri. It was the route followed by the Lewis and Clark on the Voyage of Discovery. It was laden with Montana history, possessed exceptional scenic splendor, and provided excellent riparian and upland wildlife habitat. At the field level of the Fish and Game Department, it was clear we should resist. Fort Peck Reservoir was providing all the standing water reservoir fishing we could imagine ever needing. At the same time, we knew nothing of the fish ecology of the Missouri River upstream. We needed to quickly learn what was out there in the Missouri River and on the adjacent lands that might be flooded.

Since we had no techniques available to sample such big water, we scrambled with the collecting gear we had. Gill nets and seines were employed in backwater areas and that was a start. At one adventuresome point we tried trawling as a fish-capture technique. A store-bought trawling rig was attached to a hand-cranked winch bolted to the floor of a sixteen-foot Crestliner boat powered by a 35-horsepower outboard motor. There were three of us on board for the first test run. On the very first downstream drag the net snagged some immovable object on the river bottom. This caused the boat to stop immediately and the river's strong current forced the stern of the boat to dip under water. As water rushed in, I released the brake on the hand winch, allowing the stern of the boat to rise up out of the water as the net cable screamed off the winch as we swept downstream. We were all aware of the finite length of the cable. The person at the wheel turned the boat to the bank and hit the throttle, while the third person dug out life jackets from beneath a boat seat and frantically tore at their unopened plastic wrappers. The boat heading for the bank was broadside to the river's current. When the cable hit its end, the boat rolled on its side and the river rushed in. When the cable broke free, the boat continued its rollover, with its three passengers now bobbing independently down the river.

Only two of the three had managed to get a life preserver. Nels Thoreson, the person passing out the jackets, wasn't able to get one for himself in time. He also happened to be wearing cowboy boots. The boots could not be shed and it quickly became apparent that he was going under. At that point, I pushed my life jacket to the boot-laden cowboy and quickly swam to the nearest bank. I had shed my pull-on rubber boots in the water, so now, running barefoot along the bank, I offered advice and encouragement to the two companions still bobbing downstream. As a result, a fallen cottonwood "sweeper" was avoided and the crew of three soon united on the river's bank. I had just lost a trawling net, wrecked a boat, and nearly lost my crew. A little further downstream the up-ended boat washed up on a gravel bar. It was ultimately retrieved, restored, and reused, but never again as a trawler. That idea only needed to teach its lesson once.

Efforts to learn the fish ecology of the Missouri River then focused on trapping and tagging fish that might be moving seasonally into the river's tributaries. The three tributaries with sufficient stream flows to invite and sustain fish movement were the Musselshell, Judith, and Marias rivers. Fish traps were constructed by using steel reinforcing rods to fashion a frame and funnel entrance, then covering the framework with chicken wire. That designed proved to be durable enough. The big logistical challenge was the great distances between trap sites. To inspect and maintain the traps on schedule, we would need to use a small plane.

We launched our tributary trapping project early in the spring and hauled our traps to the mouths of the rivers by truck. The most memorable trap-setting event was on the Musselshell. The river normally flowed into a large bay at the upper end of Fort Peck Reservoir. Because Fort Peck waters had been drawn down, the bay had disappeared, and the Musselshell, for the time being, flowed into the Missouri River across the bottom of the former bay. The access road ended where the bay's shoreline used to be, so now there was about a quarter mile of exposed mud flat to reach the river.

The early morning trip across that frozen mud went well. We took several hours setting the traps in the lower Musselshell and then headed back to the access road. We soon learned that the morning sun had thawed the mud flat a bit. Before long we were mired axel-deep in 30 years of accumulated silt, and as far from anywhere as we could get. The good news was that upstream ends of reservoirs accumulate a lot of wooden debris over the years. Utilizing planks and logs scavenged on site, we jacked our vehicle up out of the mud onto the corduroy road we assembled under and ahead of the truck. We then were able to drive the vehicle forward a few yards, then move the 'debris' road from behind the vehicle to ahead of it and gain a few more yards. It was sundown before we reached firm ground.

The rest of that spring was spent flying to the trap sites about three times each week, measuring, tagging, and releasing the catch. Our interest at the time was focused on walleye and sauger moving into the tributaries to spawn. To do the flying, I hired an airman/mechanic from the Glasgow Air Force Base who also had a commercial pilot's license. The plane was a Piper Super Cub and we landed on hayfields, meadows, and dry mud flats as near to our trap sites as we could get.

Since there was a lot of flying time between trap sites, the airman-pilot would spend some of it teaching me to fly. The routine became he would take off and after reaching a safe distance from other air traffic, turn the plane over to me. Since the pilot was on night shift at the airbase, he would often nap while I flew the plane between trap sites. When it was time to land, I would tap him on the shoulder, and he would wake up to put the plane safely on the ground. This became a rather dull routine—with one exception.

One day I was steering the plane back toward Glasgow over a vast tract of uninhabited river breaks and prairie. We usually flew less than a thousand feet above the ground and the drone of the Super Cub's engine was the only noise. Suddenly, without a sound, one of the huge B-52 bombers from the Glasgow Air Force Base appeared below and then ahead of us as it passed directly underneath our tiny little plane! My immediate reaction was to pull back on the stick, sending us into a steep climb, and waking the pilot. To this day I assume the pilots in that big, black, scary bomber capable of carrying nuclear bombs were having themselves a little laugh to ease the boredom of a training flight.

At about the same time a fisheries graduate student was doing a master's thesis on the life history of the goldeye fish in the Missouri River above Fort Peck Reservoir. He had been unable to collect any young-of-the-year goldeye in the river, so we agreed to help him. The plan was to set up a camp at the head of Fort Peck Reservoir and spend a week collecting young, recently hatched goldeye, if we could. Two of us from the regional office met the student and his major professor and set up camp near where C-K Creek flowed into the reservoir. We brought enough grub and beer to last about a week.

The first night it started to rain. We all knew that when the dirt roads in this part of the region became wet, their surface would turn into what the locals called "gumbo." Unlike ordinary mud, gumbo would do more than simply become slippery. Gumbo would stick to whatever it came into contact. In the case of tires, it would completely encase a tire in a large, doughnut-shaped glob. We knew we couldn't drive anywhere, but we were not concerned since we had a boat on the water, the fishing gear and food we needed, and camp was within walking distance of the shoreline. The only problem was that we drank all of the beer, except one can, on the first night.

The rain turned out to be a real soaker, and each evening we would return to camp after a day of fish collecting and stare at that lone can of beer. We were still a generation ahead of the first cell phone and no way to communicate beyond the perimeter of our camp. On the third night, one of the crew broke—and downed the lone brew. That night the rain stopped and as the new day dawned, we watched the clouds begin to breakup and scatter.

As the clouds began dispersing, we heard the drone of a small aircraft that approached and circled our camp. We soon determined it was our regional supervisor, Wes Woodgerd, checking on our welfare. We succeeded in signaling we were all okay. The plane circled back for one last pass over our camp. Just as the plane set its heading to Glasgow, five small parachutes emerged from the departing aircraft. The survival supplement thus delivered consisted of four six-packs of beer and a bundle of steaks. Some people really knew how to communicate and supervise.

In June 1964, a group of Glasgow boating enthusiasts planned a float trip down the Missouri River from Fort Benton to Fort Peck Reservoir, and then down the full length of the reservoir to the dam. Fish and Game signed up and volunteered campfire lectures on the value of a free-flowing Missouri River. While our free-river advocacy did not have the horsepower of the dam builders, we did use every means at our disposal to communicate with people at the local level.

The year of the float trip happened to be a wet spring, and the Missouri River was approaching flood stage. On the last night that we were on the river segment, we were camped in James Kipp State Park adjacent to the Fred Robinson Bridge. There were three of us in the Fish and Game crew. The night was clear so we slept in the open: two of us on military cots that held us a foot or so above the ground and our regional supervisor, Wes Woodgerd, a non-swimmer, on an air mattress on the ground between us. I happened to wake up about three in the morning and noticed that the three of us were on the same level. Fortunately Wes had not floated off in the dark. The rising river and a floating supervisor did set off a scramble. We threw all our gear and ourselves into the boat and agreed to just go with the flow. We learned later that when the day ended, all that was visible of the campground were the roofs of the outhouses. We had ridden the crest of the historic 1964 flood into the headwaters of Fort Peck Reservoir—in the dark.

The '64 flood was a whopper and it did give us a thrill on that night in June. In addition, the sheer volume of it raised the level of Fort Peck Reservoir. The rising waters covered the terrestrial vegetation that had gown on the exposed mud flats and hillsides, and in the spring of 1965 this flooded vegetation provided hundreds of miles of prime spawning and rearing habitat for yellow perch, black crappie, and northern pike.

By the mid-1960s, the Fish and Game Department was actively challenging the Corps of Engineers and trying to prevent any new dams on the Missouri River. That effort included building public support for the aesthetic, historic, recreational, and ecological values of the river. At the same time, the Corps of Engineers was rounding up civic leaders from local communities and flying them over the chosen dam sites. Some flights included a trip to their national headquarters in Omaha, Nebraska.

This entire debate over the future of the upper Missouri River was held prior to any of the environmental protection legislation that currently attends major proposed government actions. There was no National Environmental Policy Act, and there was no Montana Environmental Policy Act. There was only political will, and an appropriation from the U.S. Congress, to put the Corps of Engineers plan into action—or back on the shelf. At the time, Montana was blessed with two U. S. Senators of exceptional substance, Mike Mansfield and Lee Metcalf. As a result, there was no appropriation to build the dams. Not long after, the last un-dammed section of the Missouri River received protection under the National Wild and Scenic Rivers Act, later becoming part of the Missouri River Breaks National Monument.

The Lesson Learned On The Great Plains

When I arrived in Glasgow, a good family friend and local attorney, Bill Sternhagen, was living there. He talked me into becoming a member of the Glasgow Wranglers Kiwanis

Club. As a member of that group, time was spent on a variety of community service projects. In the process, the members of the community and I learned the values we shared. The citizens were no longer some generic form of "locals," and I became something other than a transient bureaucrat. For me, it set a pattern for the rest of my life, to become a member of both local communities and the issue-oriented public interest groups that might share my values and objectives.

As fate would have it, Bill and I moved to Helena at about the same time, he as a staff attorney in the Attorney General's office and me within the Fish and Game Department. Elk hunting became a common passion that we shared. Later, when he was in private law practice, Bill represented the Anaconda Copper Company during legislative sessions while I testified for mining law reform on the environmental side. Through it all we remained close personal friends and hunting buddies. As the years passed, members of mining groups and environmental advocates both came to label us "the odd couple."

On one occasion, I had spent a long day on the wild and scenic Missouri River with a crew from Iowa public television. Upon returning to the old Grand Union Hotel in Fort Benton around midnight, I found a note pinned to my door saying, "Call Bill Sternhagen no matter what time of day or night." Assuming there had been some sort of crises within my family, I ran down the hall to the only phone on the second story of the hotel. Upon reaching Bill, he informed me that he was chairman of the nominating committee for the upcoming election of officers for the Helena Kiwanis Club. He asked, "Would you be the second vice president?" Even though I knew that this meant I would have to be president in two years, I was so totally relieved and completely disarmed that I agreed.

The lesson learned through all of this, and other related experiences, was the importance of belonging, in real terms, to the bigger community. Thus, a tour of duty in what was the most arid part of Montana was laden with lessons taught by big waters, small communities, and solid friends.

Trout Waters and Dams

For the fisheries people, the 1960s was a decade of rolling up the sleeves and slugging it out for stream habitat conservation. Because a number of legislators visualized the Fish and Game Department shutting down highway construction with the 1963 Stream Preservation Act, the law was politically designed to expire in two years. At the time, only subdivisions of state government were required to conform with the law. One thing the wide open landscape of northeastern Montana provided was alternatives to threatening rivers with construction projects, so I had few opportunities to work on any proposals affected by the act. Considerable time, however, was devoted to running up and down the Hi-Line with colored slide shows (a primitive form of a power-point presentation) and giving speeches promoting the 1963 act as essential, while asking for public support to make it permanent. In 1965 the Stream Preservation Act sailed through both houses of the state Legislature and became permanent when signed, for the second time, by Governor Tim Babcock.

The Clark Fork River Meanders

On riverbanks all across Montana, people were making the law work as intended. One interesting story emerged when the interstate highway between Garrison and Missoula was being designed. Fish and Game argued at the outset that the Clark Fork River should be the same length after construction as it was before. This would require building two new meanders into the river to compensate for areas where channelizing and straightening the river was simply unavoidable. Two affected landowners whose property was being condemned for the new meanders took the issue to court.

The case was heard in the old, almost historic, Philipsburg courthouse. At one point the judge challenged Fish and Game witness Art Whitney, chief of the Fisheries Division. The judged asked: "If there is so much water in the river at Garrison and so much water in the river at Missoula, what difference does it make how long it takes to get there?" Since indoor plumbing had probably been added to the old building well after it was built, there were more than a few pipes visibly suspended from the ceiling. The quick-witted Whitney, using the piping as a visual aid, convinced the judge that it was the length of the pipe (or river channel habitat) that was the important factor, not the amount of water at either end. That argument prevailed and today there are two artificial meanders in the Clark Fork River between Garrison and Missoula.

The significance of that accomplishment held two gems. One jewel was that the river's length and physical habitat was preserved. The other pearl was that when this was done, the Clark Fork River was basically dead, a river polluted from marginally or untreated acid mine effluents from its headwaters in and around Butte. Today the river hosts a recovered trout population that validates the decision made decades earlier: to start habitat protection by first preserving a stream's physical features.

Art Whitney liked beer and smoked cigars. Many years later, after Art had passed away, I fished one of those artificial meanders. I brought a cigar and can of beer. As the sun left the river, I found a productive-looking backwater eddy with an occasional trout rising to feed on the hatch of the day. Taking a seat on a cottonwood log, I opened the beer, lit up the cigar, and toasted Art while savoring the beer, the cigar, the river, and the moment.

Libby Dam and the Fisher River

As the 1960s passed its midpoint, the Fish and Game Department faced a number of water development projects that threatened to impact trout waters. To address the issues, the Water Resource Development Section was added to the Fisheries Division, and I was asked to lead the unit. The family, now including Glasgow-born sons Carl and Matthew, packed up and moved to Helena.

Shortly after arriving in Helena, I enrolled in a creative writing class at Carroll College. My previous formal education included rigid training relative to collecting and reporting scientific information. There was no room for expressing opinions, much less emotions, relative to the issues and places being dealt with. The trouble was that I cared about the resources and places we were dealing with, and I felt the need to break out of the rigid mold. We were dealing with public resources in a democracy, so the need to communicate went well beyond the scientific community.

At the top of the list of pressing issues was Libby Dam, a Corps of Engineers project under way on the Kootenai River in northwest Montana. The project's two major impacts were the flooding of critical wildlife habitat with the reservoir, and severe channelization of the adjacent Fisher River. Since the U.S. Army Corps of Engineers was a federal agency, they were not subject to provisions of Montana's Stream Preservation Act. There was a federal Fish and Wildlife Coordination Act that required the Corps to consult with the U.S. Fish and Wildlife Service, but "consultation" was all that was required. The net effect was that little would happen to avoid or compensate for damaged fish and wildlife habitat unless the Corps decided it was convenient and not too expensive.

While there was considerable bureaucratic activity going on as Libby Dam was planned and moved into construction, there was little public awareness of its impact on fish and wildlife. Since Montana Fish and Game was doing little more than commenting from the bureaucratic sidelines, a new strategy was developed. We took our message directly to the people. Since fighting the Corps of Engineers within the government wasn't working, we once again took our fight to the street.

At this point in history, we had two major battles and a number of local conflicts going on with the Corps of Engineers. The dam builders were still pressing for two additional dams on the Missouri River, there was the Libby Dam and the associated relocation of the Great Northern Railroad, and there was a proposal to realign and high-bank the Big Hole River to fit it under a bridge. Our objective was to expose what was going on. Using Fish and Game media outlets, we attacked the Corps of Engineers.

In an article titled "Fate of the Wild Missouri—or, Pork Barrel, Pigs and Peas," I compared what the Corps of Engineers was implying might happen when talking to the public, with what was actually in their plan. Our illustrator drew a great political cartoon of a hustler engaged in the old "shell game." In another article titled "Ravage the River," we included statements of then President Lyndon Johnson taken from his 1965 State of the Union address. The statements extolled the beauty and importance of our nation's natural places. We printed them over pictures of the Corps of Engineers devastating the Fisher River.

While all this was going on, there was a proposal brought

forward to channel the Big Hole River just upstream from a county bridge. At one point, one of the county commissioners called and asked why we were objecting and why the Corps of Engineers was so afraid of me. After explaining that our objective was to protect fish habitat, I said about all we could do to influence the Corps was to "burn 'em" with public exposure when they damaged fish and wildlife habitat. The commissioner then set up a public debate between a Corps representative and me. It was a meeting typical of the times, a sea of cowboy hats filling the room from podium to the back door. The Corps of Engineers representative had a speech so short I can still remember it. He said, "Whatever you guys want to do out there we will be happy to do it for you." That was it, his entire speech! The county commissioner then introduced me saying that I "would begin by explaining the 'burning process.'" I was on my feet for a good while, but the stream channel ultimately survived, at least for a while.

While these various debates were going on, the Corps of Engineers contracted with the University of Montana to have them give some of their people "sensitivity training." Dr. Les Pengelly, wildlife professor at the university, drew the assignment. Dr. Pengelly, who was a good friend and an incorrigible humorist, invited me to give a lecture to the group. I soon learned he had also picked a title for my talk. When he introduced me he said, "... and the title of Jim's presentation will be 'Rotten to the Corps.'"

An Interstate Intersection and Stream Preservation

One of the more dramatic episodes in implementing the stream preservation act occurred in the early 1970s. Montana's North/South interstate highway is I-15. Our East/West interstate is I-90. Needless to say, those two major transportation corridors needed to intersect somewhere. It was assumed there would be significant economic potential or impact where that intersection was located. The proposed location was Butte. The problem with that selection was that I-15 north of Butte would have to be stuffed in the Boulder River Canyon, and there was already a primary highway, railroad, and trout river there. We took a shot at challenging the location.

The Montana Environmental Policy Act had become law in 1971 but had yet to be applied to highway routing. We began by advocating that an environmental impact statement be written and that it consider alternative routes for I-15. That action set off quite a political storm. A former Fish and Game Department Director was running an environmental consulting firm and was engaged to promote the Butte location as the proper alignment.

During the debate that quickly escalated, a person who was the liaison between Montana's U.S. Senators and the state government showed up in the Fish and Game Director's office. His mission was to find out what we thought we were doing. The director invited me to participate in the discussion. During the course of the conversation the liaison informed us that the U.S. Senators promised Butte the interstate intersection. In response I said, "You know, the Anaconda Copper Company used to get everything they wanted but they were just denied an easement that would have let them dam Alice Creek to facilitate an open pit mine at the head of the Blackfoot River. So now they know they no longer get everything they want. And the state legislature just passed a utility siting act so Montana Power just learned they don't get everything they want."

I then concluded by saying, "Maybe it's time somebody told Butte they don't get everything they want anymore!" The liaison leaned over the table, looked me square in the eye, and in a whisper said, "*You* tell 'em." Then he got up and left the room.

It wasn't long before the Butte Rotary Club invited me to make a presentation on our position on the routing of Interstate 15. I had made a previous presentation to the Butte Rotary in January 1970, three months prior to America's first Earth Day. The agency had recently created the Environmental Resources Division and I was appointed its administrator. The title of that first presentation was "The Fish and Game Department and the Environment."

When we challenged the interstate alignment, the city of Butte had formed an I-15 Task Force to represent their interest. The Rotary Club met in the old uptown Finlen Hotel which was the center of Butte social life and a pretty fancy place at the time. Right below the speaker's podium they had set up a round table around which the Butte and Anaconda state legislators were seated. The Butte I-15 Task Force was well represented.

My presentation in 1973 started with a slide show illustrating the damage done to our trout streams prior to the 1963 and 1965 stream preservation acts. I described the details of the act and the public trust that we held as its administrators. Nearing the end of the presentation I quoted Theodore Roosevelt's "Man in the Arena" speech while pointing out that nowhere in the law were we instructed to "take a dive" if it got too hot in the kitchen. Then I closed with the following:

In opening up this discussion for comments or questions from the group, I would like to close with one more quote. I can't tell you its author, since I believe I first saw it on the wall of a men's room. It says, "God will not look you over for medals, degrees, or diplomas, but for scars." I have a feeling you are about to improve my acceptability to the Lord!

It was then open season, and the Butte Rotarians had the opportunity to express themselves consistent with the unique character of their community. Their response was civil and not nearly as rough as I had expected, but it was clear they were determined to have those interstate highways intersect in Butte.

While speaking to the Rotarians I also had a fisheries crew sampling headwater streams along the proposed interstate alignment between Basin and Elk Park. The purpose was to measure the potential of those headwater streams to produce trout upstream from the old mine tailings and acid drainages that retarded trout populations downstream. On the way back to Helena, with a couple of six packs aboard, I located the crew and we shared a brew streamside. It helped salve the wounds while they were still fresh.

The net effect of this effort was that the governor informed us the interstate intersection would be in Butte, and the highway department would do what Fish and Game asked to minimize the damage to the river. Thus, the interstate south of Boulder begins with a split alignment somewhat sheltering the river that now runs between the north- and south-bound lanes. There are also numerous bridges to accommodate the limited stream meandering that can occur in the narrow canyon. In addition, the curvature standards for interstate highways were compromised in deference to stream alignment. Thanks to the dogged persistence of biologist Ralph Boland, the Fish and Game Department's representative on this project, the river received as much protection as possible under the circumstances.

Some twenty years after my second appearance at the Butte Rotary, I received an invitation to appear once again. By this time the grand old Finlen Hotel had faded from its former grandeur and the club was meeting in the dining room of a motel on the town's commercial strip. After making a good-humored presentation about my prior appearance in 1973, we all enjoyed a few laughs and pleasantries. Upon my conclusion, a rather elderly gentleman stood up at the back of the room and, shaking his finger at me, loudly proclaimed, "I remember that meeting, we called you young man!"

The Conservation Horizon Expands

The decade of the 1960s was a busy time for the Montana Department of Fish and Game. During that time, the agency firmly assumed a focus on habitat protection and acquisition. Governor Tim Babcock, who signed the two stream preservation laws, finished his second term and was succeeded by Forest H. Anderson, who campaigned on reorganizing state government. That reorganization would have a profound effect on the Fish and Game Department. The political battles that ensued during the Anderson administration (1970-1973) saw the department's director, Frank Dunkle, resign and enter the political arena to run for governor as a Republican as the "Green Wave" of environmental awakening was sweeping the country. Anderson chose not to seek reelection. The Montana Republican Party, however, chose to eliminate Dunkle in their primary. In the general election, Democrat Thomas L. Judge was elected. He would be the first governor to appoint a Fish and Game Director who would serve at the pleasure of the governor's office.

The focus of the political discourse and tension throughout Anderson's term had been the political determination to make all agency directors political appointees. Prior to reorganization, the director of Fish and Game was a qualified professional hired by the Fish and Game Commission. The director was a state employee, and as such, that person could only be removed from office for "just cause." It was a relationship established broadly across the nation following the conservation reformation triggered by Franklin D. Roosevelt's first North American Wildlife Conference in the mid-1930s. The design was developed specifically to keep politics out of fish and wildlife management. With the passage of time and the dramatic restoration of fish and wildlife populations, they once again became public assets of considerable economic value and potential. As a result, political tolerance of agency independence began to erode, all across the United States. The political struggle was bitter, but in the end Fish and Game had to conform to the new system. Henceforth, the Fish and Game Director would serve at the pleasure of the governor, and there would be no specified job qualifications.

The director's position remained a protracted struggle that spanned the 1970s. In that time period, two individuals served as Montana governor and five people passed through as director of Fish and Game. Tom Judge's first selection of a director was career Fish and Game biologist and manager, Wes Woodgerd. In the four years that followed, the governor learned that Wes saw his job as being the defender of the agency and its conservation advocacy. In Judge's second term he selected an academic who had to be replaced when he ran off with a typewriter and entered drug rehab. It was reported that this director was asked at a public meeting what it was like to be the head of Fish and Game. His response was, "I know I have the steering wheel in my hand, but I don't think it is connected to anything."

The agency professionals in the field were apolitical and dedicated to a mission growing more critical as pressure escalated on fish, wildlife, and wild places. While the political struggle occupied the agency leadership, events in the field and in Montana society in general presented significant challenges and opportunities. America was turning "Green."

Earth Day was just around the corner, and environmental policy acts were emerging on the national and state levels. All of these trends would give fish and wildlife agencies more opportunities to represent the needs of fish and wildlife.

While the fisheries workers were protecting the physical habitat, they and the agency continued advocating for other essential reforms. The 1964 flood had revived a host of dam building proposals including: Sun Butte, Castle Reef, and Lowery on the Sun River; Spruce Park on the Middle Fork of the Flathead River; Glacier View on the North Fork of the Flathead River; and Reichle on the Big Hole River. The conservation community, including efforts by John and Frank Craighead, produced the federal Wild and Scenic Rivers Act, signed by President Lyndon B. Johnson in 1968. None of the proposed dams were built.

Perhaps the most dramatic event reflecting the growing environmental sensitivity of the times was a request for an easement on state lands in the upper Blackfoot River watershed. On Christmas Eve, 1969, the Anaconda Copper Company requested an easement on State School Trust Lands to build a dam and impound Alice Creek. The water was needed to develop the Heddleson Mining District as a new open pit copper/molybdenum mine. On March 2, 1970, the Montana State Land Board consisting of the Governor, the Attorney General, the Secretary of State, and the Superintendant of Public Instruction met to consider the request.

Feeling some of the new environmental pressure, the Land Board asked a handful of state agencies to prepare a list of conditions that might be attached to the easement. Fish and Game was a part of that group and the initial conditions proposed were:

1. The easement be revoked ... upon a finding ...
that the Anaconda Company is in violation of...
existing pollution control standards ... in the Lincoln
(Heddleston) area."
2. That on the termination of revocation of this
easement, the Anaconda Company agrees to reclaim
the land to its best beneficial use.
3. That on the termination or revocation of this
easement, the Anaconda Company agrees to assure
perpetual maintenance of clarification ponds or other
structures on these tracts.

These recommendations were read into the record at
the March 2nd meeting. This was immediately followed by
Secretary of State Frank Murray reading into the minutes
a list of major expenditures the Anaconda Company made
in Montana in 1969. Governor Anderson followed in turn
by reading letters and telegrams from Senator Mansfield
reviewing conversations and promises resulting from meetings
with company officials in Washington D.C. At least half the
State Land Board was following the old script.

While the public was expressing concern relative to
the mines impact on the river, they had little formal space
open to them. On this day, however, the meeting room was
packed wall to wall with people there to express opposition
to the project. For the most part they were students from
the University of Montana. The State Land Board had never
experienced anything like it. The meeting soon fell off the
script that it had followed since the dawn of Montana's
Copper Kings. The Governor and Secretary of State were
obviously angry as they read their portion of the Company
script. *Missoulian* outdoor writer Dale Burk noted in his

March 8, 1970, "Outdoor Picture" column that "Anderson...
and Murray both sounded like board members of the
Anaconda Company as they naively questioned the company
about the project—never once asking...pointed questions
to seek information of environmental worth." The normally
cool company lawyers stammered and struggled as they were
pressed into thinking on their feet rather than the old pattern
of just following a script. The net effect at the end of the
day was a motion by Attorney General Robert Woodall to
postpone consideration of granting the easement, which was
seconded by Superintendant of Public Instruction Deloris
Colburg, and passed. The easement, on that day at least, was
denied. Two of Montana's mythical yet traditional "copper
collars" pinged as they hit the floor of the meeting room in
the state Capitol which was, then as now, domed with a roof
of copper.

Following that meeting, Fish and Game Director Frank
Dunkle called me into his office and told me he had been
confronted by Governor Anderson who emphatically told
him, "You caused this @#$%&! mess, now you solve it!" Frank
then told me the Water Resource Development Section of the
Fisheries Division was being elevated to the Environmental
Resources Division. In addition to our existing stream habitat
and water development duties, we would now address the
broadening environmental horizon. America's first Earth Day,
April 22, 1970, was still 50 days away.

On the personal side, as my conservation agenda was
expanding, so was my family with its final member, Andrew,
being born the same year the Environmental Resources
Division was formed.

On May 20, 1970, the Montana State Land Board again
met to consider the easement. In the interim, state agencies

and the Anaconda Company had been meeting to discuss the proposed conditions and the necessary database that would have to be collected. By this time the list of conditions had grown from three to eleven, and the board requested the company to express "by letter of intent…to communicate and cooperate…concerning all other present and contemplated Anaconda Company operations in Montana."

In order to meet the conditions now laid before the company, considerable work needed to be done. From the Fish and Game perspective we needed a credible database relative to the fish populations at the head of the Blackfoot River and to elk use on a place called Spencer Bar which would be affected if the mine were developed. We offered the Anaconda Company a cooperative fish and wildlife inventory that we would conduct if they would put up $10,000 to fund half the cost. When I met with a company representative to address the details, we met over lunch in the dining room of the old Finlen Hotel. That meeting started with the company representative informing me of certain rules I needed to be aware of. They would contribute the money we were asking for, and they would pay for lunch. However, company policy limited each person to no more than two martinis at lunch. Thus informed, we launched the fish and wildlife study of the mine site and associated water resources—and skipped the martinis.

In the process of considering the proposed terms of the Alice Creek easement, the Anaconda Copper Company discovered they didn't need Alice Creek water after all. While our field staff continued gathering the data that Anaconda helped fund, Chile's Marxist President Salvador Allende nationalized the company's lucrative mines in that country and drove them to the brink of bankruptcy. They were then swallowed by a fiscally stronger mining company, Atlantic Richfield.[9] Through it all, copper prices fell, and the idea of an open pit copper mine in the Blackfoot River headwaters dried up. The next time a trout rises to your fly on this treasure of a river, you might take pause to thank Salvador.

Once again the take-home message of the Blackfoot River saga was to put trust and faith in the Montana people. Those students who showed up and stood up at the State Land Board meeting changed the course of environmental history. It wasn't long after they drew their "green line" in the sand that others rallied to the cause of the river. They included groups like Trout Unlimited, local Lincoln residents such as Cecil Garland, the Montana Wildlife Federation, and a couple of the federation's student interns who soon formed the Montana Environmental Information Center, Phil and Robin Tawney. Although the Anaconda Copper Company vanished into the corporate blender, the people who hold the Montana conservation ethic are still defending this precious waterway, and renewing themselves by the generation.

Subsequent environmental legislation produced funds to clean up some residual pollution left behind by various mining ventures in the Blackfoot area dating back to the late 1800s. The ore body that will forever call to miners and financiers, like the Sirens called to Ulysses, remains.

The battle for the Blackfoot echoes to this day. My fourth son Carl grew up and became an architect and created a company to design and build things in Missoula and beyond. On August 13, 2017, forty-seven years after the battle prevented an open pit mine at head of this treasured river, western singer Lyle Lovett and his big band dedicated

[9] Malone, Michael. "Close of a Copper Century." *Great Falls Tribune,* August 18, 1985.

Montana's first amphitheater. It sits near the Blackfoot's union with the Clark Fork River in Bonner. Carl's firm designed it, and he invited my wife and me to attend. In the course of the evening, a tall blonde lady came over and gave me a huge hug. Her name was Bobbie Sue Tilton, and she was from Tiger Butte, just south of Belt. That night she spotted me from across the amphitheater. Bobbie Sue was the youngest daughter of Nels Thoreson, my boss and mentor when I took my first step in Fish and Game—a half century and six years prior. My fledgling family spent many weekends at the Thoreson ranch where Nels taught me that fence wire was strung tight and friendships loose. Bobbie Sue's mom, Kathleen, fed us like we were royalty and made us part of the family. That brief reunion with Bobbie Sue turned a pretty special event into a truly glorious evening, costing an old man more than a few tears.

From our seats in the amphitheater we could see a piece of the Blackfoot River and took note of a red canoe pulled up on the bank. After the concert we spotted the red canoe in midstream with a couple aboard, presumably heading for home. It is truly amazing how these rivers, with tributaries and side channels, just keep running through us.

A Political Reformation

Montana's fish and wildlife conservation ethic has deep and persistent roots that surface occasionally in political action. They are actions to protect fish and wildlife such as those taken by the Stuart brothers as early Territorial Legislators. These were actions taken by Montana pioneers before Custer died on the hills above the Little Bighorn River. In more recent times, the first stream habitat protection laws of the early 1960s introduced the idea of legislating habitat protection as a fundamental social and cultural objective. When the "Earth Decade" of the 1970s approached, there was a dramatic expansion of that idea. Powerful crosscurrents flowed through our social community and out across the landscape. In addition to the action on the upper Blackfoot River, large blocks of mineral claims were being taken all across Montana from the Cabinets to the Beartooths. Coal strip mining was going through an awakening, and in the middle of it all, the Arab oil embargo sent gas prices soaring.

As the frenetic 1970s arrived, environmental protection laws were marginal to non-existent. For coal companies, the surface mining reclamation law was simple enough: the mining companies could reclaim the land if they wanted to, and if they did, they would get a tax benefit. Hard rock mine reclamation law was unheard of. Water could not be claimed or maintained in streams for the benefit of fish except for sections of our best blue-ribbon trout streams. A law to prohibit the dredge mining of trout streams was passed in 1969, but it was later ruled unconstitutional. The need for change was overpowering. The people knew it and those who represented them responded.

Over the stretch of Montana legislative sessions from 1969 through 1975, surface mine law evolved from voluntary reclamation to one of the most stringent laws in the nation. By mid-decade reclamation was mandatory and required reshaping spoils, retention and re-use of top-soil, planting of native plant species, and selective denial of ecologically critical sites. A Hard Rock Mining Reclamation law followed with a policy requiring "proper reclamation of mined land…to prevent…conditions detrimental to the general welfare, health, safety, ecology and property rights of the citizens of the state." The Montana Water Quality Act was totally revamped and it included the protection of "wildlife, fish and aquatic life." A new water law passed with provisions for reserving in-stream flows for fish and wildlife. A state nongame and endangered species act was passed. A comprehensive utility siting act was passed that required a certificate of need and environmental compatibility before a major energy conversion facility could be built; assessing that compatibility included effects on fish and wildlife. There also was the Montana Environmental Policy Act and a new State Constitution giving Montana citizens the right to "a clean and healthful environment."

The list of positive legal changes in this period could go on. The point of all of them was the same: fish, wildlife, and their habitats were recognized and made legitimate public values to be represented. Few of these laws required Fish and Game participation, but all of them invited it, leaving the initiative to the Fish and Game Commission and Department. Those of us with the public trust responsibility to nurture and protect fish and wildlife were invited to the table. Howling at those mauling the environment, or trying to "burn 'em" with nasty editorials, were no longer our only options.

This reformation happened because there was a basic conservation ethic in the people, and it was reflected in their elected officials, whether they were liberal or conservative in their political ideology. Equally important, the reformation was possible because the political climate was not polarized. Unfortunately, before the 1970s would end, exploitive interests were creating a more polarized electorate. All environmentalists suddenly were branded as extremists, and vilifying the messenger replaced addressing the message. As time passed, some provisions in the new body of conservation law were modified. However, much was retained, and some of it was applied to the monumental struggle that occurred next: Montana's coal fields and the 670-mile free-flowing river that runs through it, the Yellowstone. That trip, like rafting through the Yellowstone's Yankee Jim Canyon, was quite the ride!

Coal and the Yellowstone River

The Social-Political Environment

Yellowstone was America's first national park, designated on March 1, 1872. This premier park became part of our American culture four years before Colonel George Armstrong Custer and the U.S. 7th Cavalry bit the dust in 1876 on the hills above the Little Bighorn River, a tributary of the Yellowstone. The same year 80,000 buffalo hides were shipped down the Missouri River from Fort Benton. It was a record high, and, in a way, that is what the battle was about. A mere ten years later, in 1886, the U.S. 1st Cavalry rode into Yellowstone National Park to protect the last few dozen wild buffalo left alive in the United States.

Within the park, the North Fork and South Fork of the Yellowstone River merge and feed Yellowstone Lake. After the river leaves the lake, it crashes 109 feet over Upper Yellowstone Falls, thunders 308 feet over Lower Yellowstone Falls, tumbles 24 miles through the Grand Canyon of the Yellowstone, and enters Montana at Gardiner. Then it churns through Yankee Jim Canyon, calms a bit, and meanders through a broad intermountain valley we have always called Paradise. The river continues hundreds of miles to its confluence with the Missouri River just beyond Montana's eastern border with North Dakota.

In 1972, exactly 100 years after the park was created, three biologists of the Environmental Resources Division of the Montana Fish and Game Department drove into Paradise Valley. A year prior to that, the U.S. Bureau of Reclamation in collaboration with some of the nation's biggest utilities and power producers released the "North Central Power Study." The study called for 42 coal-fired power plants to be built on the coal fields of southeast Montana and northeast Wyoming, and those plants were to be cooled by water from the Yellowstone River.

A companion plan, the "Montana Wyoming Aqueduct Study," suggested delivering roughly one-third of the river's average flow to cool those plants, slurry a bit of coal elsewhere, and perhaps throw in a coal-gasification plant or two. The aqueduct study noted that there would be enough water to do all this if a "storage facility" was built at the Allenspur site just south of Livingston. Of course, the "storage facility" was a major dam.

At the same time, major coal-mining corporations were acquiring coal leases in eastern Montana. It was obvious that another battle over Allenspur was inevitable. In preparation, biologists Larry Peterman, Bob Martinka, and Kerry Constan were dispatched to measure the fish and wildlife values of Paradise Valley and the river that ran through it.

As this preliminary positioning was occurring, the Fish and Game's Environmental Resources Division was reorganized into the Environment and Information Division. The reorganization merged the department's two smallest divisions. The purpose was to achieve efficiency through reduced administrative overhead. The real-world effect was that it combined the agency's public communication and education capacity with its environmental advocacy team. It would prove to be a critical move and its timing could not have been better. In the process, I became and would serve as the only division administrator the unit would ever have.

At the political and legal level there were few tools

available for river advocacy. A 1969 law allowed the Fish and Game Department to claim an in-stream water right on portions of Montana's top "Blue Ribbon" trout streams and that had been done. Efforts to have the Yellowstone River become part of the National Wild and Scenic River System were unsuccessful. An attempt to create a state wild and scenic river system failed to receive legislative approval. However, the brand new Montana State Constitution stated: "The state and each person shall maintain and improve a clean and healthful environment in Montana for present and future generations."

While this constitutional recognition held promise, we had not yet learned what conservation tools it might produce. Then, while those three biologists were working through their first year of gathering fish and wildlife baseline inventories, everything changed.

In October 1973, Arab oil-producing countries cut off oil shipments to the United States to protest American support for Israel in its 1973 Yom Kippur War with Egypt and Syria. That, in turn, triggered gas shortages, high gas prices, and a general economic downturn. Starting in November 1973, President Richard Nixon began presenting his plan for energy independence. The plan included an important role for surface mining. The "North Central Power Study" and massive coal development of the Northern Great Plains took on a new possibility. The conversational language of the times included terms such as: "the boiler room of the nation, national sacrifice area, Appalachia West, resist and you will freeze to death in the dark." The nation's energy industry and the main federal dam-building agency had just been energized and invigorated by the President of the United States. In defense of fish and wildlife, we countered with three biologists in the field and a state agency's public information capacity.

While the Yellowstone River failed to pick up protective legislation as a wild and scenic river, the Montana Legislature was well aware of the controversy and the need. People at the grassroots level formed "The Allenspur Committee to Save the Upper Yellowstone." This group and others kept the issue front and center while the Legislature focused on passing a near total revision of Montana water law. Provisions of that law, passed in 1973, listed fish, wildlife, and recreation as beneficial uses of water and allowed, for the first time, state agencies to apply to the Montana Department of Natural Resources and Conservation (DNRC) for an in-stream flow allocation. In addition, the 1974 state Legislature placed a three-year moratorium on major industrial water withdrawals from the Yellowstone River.

Suddenly, for those of us working on the issue at Fish and Game, the challenge swelled. It exploded from the thirty-some miles of Yellowstone River flowing through Paradise Valley to 670 miles of a free-flowing river running from Gardiner to its union with the Missouri River north of Sidney. We now had a chance to make a claim on the Yellowstone for fish, wildlife, and recreation. This time we had to not only recognize and strive to meet the need of the Yellowstone cutthroat trout of Paradise, but also the mysterious paddlefish of the lower Yellowstone. Fossil evidence suggested the paddlefish had been waiting for a little recognition and acceptance since the Late Cretaceous.

Due to progressive, bi-partisan, and conservation-focused legislative actions possible at the time, we were invited, or challenged, to look at the whole thing. At the administrative level that meant finding the money to hire the essential field biologists to gather information, coordinate with existing agency field staff already spread along the river, and pass the

Proposed Allenspur Dam site in the Paradise Valley *(Photo by Gayle Joslin)*

incoming information to those in closest communication with the people of Montana. This latter step was recognized as absolutely critical. We had just changed Montana water law from the relatively simple model that required taking water out of a stream to establish a right to use it, to a more complex model that suggested leaving water in-stream was not only okay, but also legal and perhaps even a good idea.

We now had to gather field data to convince the Board of Natural Resources and Conservation to dedicate an in-stream flow reservation to fish and wildlife. Perhaps more important, we also had to convince a rural population that the traditional slogan/cliché to "Use It or Lose It" also meant using water by leaving it in the stream to sustain natural systems. Both of these objectives would require additional resources to cover the costs of more people spread over a broad ecological and social landscape. That would take money.

Through most of its history, Fish and Game operated on revenue obtained from hunting and fishing license fees, fines, and excise taxes collected on the sale of firearms, ammunition, and fishing tackle. Since those funding sources were stable and already allocated throughout the agency's traditional programs, new revenue had to be secured. We broke the old mold when we collaborated with the Anaconda Company in 1969 to put a fish and wildlife biologist in the field on the proposed mine at the head of the Blackfoot River. Given the attention that the energy crisis 1973-74 attracted, we took the Blackfoot model and offered our service as a contractor to secure essential fish and wildlife data to both government agencies and corporate entities now swarming over the coal fields.

The rapidly evolving set of state and federal laws, including the National Environmental Policy Act, a state Environmental Policy Act, the new Montana Water Use Act, the 1974 Yellowstone River Water Use Moratorium, and the 1975 Major Facility Siting Act, all required fish and wildlife representation. These laws, plus our public trust responsibility, mandated or at least encouraged our participation. We believed the cost of taking our advocacy to this higher plain needed to be shared by those who posed the threat to the land and water. As a practical matter, we simply could not finance internally what needed to be done.

As a result, the Old West Regional Commission became one of our major funders. The Commission was a federally funded organization consisting of a federal co-chairman and the governors of six western states, including Montana. We also received federal financial support from the Bureau of Reclamation, the Environmental Protection Agency, and the U.S. Fish and Wildlife Service. From the private sector,

Colorado Interstate Gas, Panhandle Eastern, Intake Water Company, and Utah International all provided financial assistance. The net effect of the funding was an ability to put people on the river and its floodplain to learn and then tell the river's story.

The River

The warm, nutrient-rich hot springs in Yellowstone National Park give the Yellowstone River a head start over most other western streams that are born of high country snow melt and in a few cases even glaciers. Those nutrients begin the cycle of life-nurturing algae and other aquatic life. The research conducted through the 1970s began there. The effort then moved up the food chain to include segments on insects, fish, migratory birds, furbearers, other wildlife of the fertile river bottom, and even the needs of soaring eagles that honored us with their presence. Human recreational use of the river was viewed as a component of the ecosystem and included. These studies became the foundation for the Fish and Game Department's application to the Montana DNRC for an in-stream flow reservation. On November 1, 1976, the applications for in-stream flow reservations were due no later than 5:00 p.m.. At 4:55 p.m. Fish and Game biologist Liter Spence walked into the DNRC office with an application for 8.2 million acre feet of water for an in-stream flow reservation in the Yellowstone River and its main tributaries. The average annual flow of the river was around 8.8 million acre feet.

Most of the field biologists who worked on the contract studies were relatively young, some on their first professional job out of college. They and other agency contributors were soon thrown into several months of contested hearings and public debate. The in-stream application was quickly challenged by hired technicians and some of the best water lawyers in the state who represented the coal and power industries. The hearings in the fall of 1977 produced 10,000 pages of documents and boxes of scientific evidence to review. During the hearing, 24 biologists and associated scientists would defend the application through sometimes brutal cross examination. I was well aware that most of us in this profession came to it with the idea of disappearing into forest and stream and living in quiet seclusion. Now I was throwing rookies into an environment that was exactly what they probably sought to avoid. The months-long hearings did produce a few of golden moments.

While the biologists were thus engaged, the education/information component of the team was in full harness pulling a huge share of the load. The biologists were assembling a solid information base defining and describing this remarkable river. At the same time, information people were disseminating those findings, perspectives, and the feelings of those engaged in this battle through every available outlet. We fully understood the reality of having to swing broad public opinion from the old "use it or lose it" water-law mindset to "it is the river that matters." This effort likewise produced its own golden moments.

The Contested Hearings

The hearings on the in-stream flow applications were held in Billings starting in late summer of 1977. Our team of biologists and technicians was housed in summertime vacant dorm rooms at what was then Eastern Montana College. All applicants for water reservations were represented by counsel. Likewise, those interests seeking water for industrial and other purposes were there to argue their position and to challenge other applicants. Most formidable among them were lawyers from Utah International and Intake Water Company. Both were seasoned attorneys and among the most respected water-right lawyers in the state. Both corporations had made claim to water from the Powder River and were also litigating among themselves to try and establish priorities. Now their focus shifted to preventing the Fish and Game from getting an in-stream flow reservation that could preclude either of them from claiming Powder River water and from drying up the Powder.

The Powder River's Golden Moment

The Powder River was the perfect place to test Montana's commitment to stream conservation. This tributary of the Yellowstone drains arid parts of Montana and Wyoming. Because it carried a heavy load of silt, the stream had the reputation of "being too thick to drink and too thin to plow." Coal reserves in the Powder Basin were enormous. Federal energy planners, giant energy production corporations, and at least one President of the United States were beating on the "dig and develop" drum. We responded by hiring a young fishery biologist to go out there and take a look. It was his first job as he graduated Montana State University with a Master's Degree in Fish and Wildlife Management.

The young biologist was Bruce Rehwinkel. His baseline inventory documented a variety of fish tolerant of warmer waters including sauger, walleye, catfish, and shovelnose sturgeon. The baseline data also described the lower Powder River's relationship with fish seasonally migrating out of the Yellowstone. His work documented the quantity of water needed to preserve these fish. In addition, Bruce learned there was a tiny silt-tolerant fish that really liked the Powder, perhaps better than any other Montana stream. It was the sturgeon chub. The what?

While most of us working on this vast watershed draining one-third of Montana had caught and savored Yellowstone cutthroat trout, I don't think any of us had ever seen or heard of the sturgeon chub *(Macrhybopsis gelida)*. If an angler ever managed to catch one longer than three and a half inches, it would have to be considered a trophy worth mounting. However little *Macrhybopsis* was out there, Bruce had found them, and they too deserved our best shot. We were well aware that the two toughest lawyers working over our witnesses were there because of their clients' interest in the Powder River's water. It was to my greatest satisfaction that no one on the team ever suggested we take a dive on the Powder and drop it from the in-stream flow process. Contrary to the old traditional western cliché and advice, we were determined to "keep our Powder wet."

Throughout the contested hearing process, we would spend evenings working with each of our witnesses prior to their testimony and cross examination the next day. This informal briefing usually involved myself and Mona Jamison, who was the attorney for the Montana Department of Health. That agency had requested in-stream reservations to assure enough water in the Yellowstone to adequately dilute treated, partially treated, and untreated discharges from cities and from agricultural return flows.

When it came Bruce's turn, we anticipated some of the most intense cross examination challenging his findings and his analysis. During the evening preparation, both Mona and I agreed the opponents would try and deride the status of the Powder River. Throughout previous questionings, references were frequently made to Montana's "Blue Ribbon Streams."

This trademark was the result of Fish and Game's formal classification of its very best trout waters as Blue Ribbon Streams long before this particular battle. We agreed that there was a need to reduce the tension that had been building in anticipation of this specific cross-examination. I thought what the whole thing needed was a little humor to break the tension. We all anticipated the opponents would ask whether or not any part of the Powder was a Blue Ribbon stream. Well, we formulated an answer.

The next morning, Bruce, showing a bit of anxiety, took the stand and swore to tell the whole truth as had the other witnesses. It wasn't long before one of the corporate lawyers got stare-in-the-face close to Bruce and posed the anticipated question. It was something like: "Now Mr. Rehwinkel, the Powder River is not really one of your Blue Ribbon Streams is it?" Bruce turned toward me, our eyes met, and with an extended index finger I pointed right at him. Without hesitation Bruce looked back at the attorney and said: "No, but I think it is on its way to becoming Montana's first 'Black and Blue Ribbon Stream!'" The chamber erupted in laughter, the tension was broken, and Bruce cruised through his cross-examination. It was the Powder River's golden moment.

After the hearings were over, I gathered a couple of *Macrhybopsis* and placed each three and a half inch specimen in a tiny glass tube of preservative. I sent one to the attorney for Utah International and the other to the attorney representing the Intake Water Company. I did not hear back from either of them so I will never know if these trophy sized *Macrhybopsis* were taken as slap-on-the-back humor or poke-in-your-eye nasty.

There was one other golden moment in this protracted hearing process worth telling. I was the last of the more than twenty witnesses being called to testify in support of the in-stream flow reservation. The prior night, Mona Jamison and I were going over my prepared testimony and speculating how the cross-examination might go. Well, this was 1977 and the movie *Star Wars* was new and playing locally. Most of us had seen the film while we were tied down at the hearing. As we were concluding our preparation I told Mona: "Tomorrow, from the witness chair, I will call upon 'The Force' to be with me." We both had a laugh and called it a day.

The next day I was being grilled by the attorney representing the Montana Power Company. He had also been the state's attorney general. He started on me by trying to establish that I was personally responsible for pursuing the in-stream reservation for fish and wildlife. It is essential to appreciate that Mona, a very sharp, intense, and focused person, was hanging on every word in the witness/lawyer exchange. The power company lawyer began by trying to establish that neither the Fish and Game Commission nor the agency director really authorized our pursuit of an in-stream allocation. His questioning kept asserting that "this is something you did on your own, isn't it?" Finally, after the third or fourth time around on this point, I saw and took the opportunity. There were a couple of rows of Fish and Game witnesses and supporters seated together on one side of the hearing room. Gesturing toward them with a swing of my arm I responded, "I didn't do this alone, this whole 'Force' was with me." There were only two people in the crowed hearing room that had any way of knowing what had just been pulled off. Mona was one of them and instantly she let out an audible shriek that was half scream and half cheer that surprised, stunned, and silenced all present. After a muttered "Sorry Mr. hearing examiner, excuse me sir, etc.,

etc." or something to that effect, the hearing resumed. For two of us however, we had a private golden moment and more important, "The Force" was now with us.

The hearings filled boxes with testimony and evidence that was studied and analyzed for more than a year as the Board of Natural Resources and Conservation deliberated. The hearings represented a finish line of sorts for those studying the ecology of the Yellowstone River system. The public education effort continued and if anything intensified. The biologists had produced a treasure trove of information. That information now had to be used to develop a public consensus that the river's health was more desirable than the economic boom promised by forty-two coal-fired power plants and the draining of the Yellowstone River to become cooling water for those plants.

The Public Information Campaign

The public information component of Fish and Game's Environment and Information Division had no additional monetary resources to throw into the battle for the Yellowstone. Nonetheless, they responded to the challenge. They focused their educational outreach on the Yellowstone and the growing body of information produced by the field biologists. The outreach included lectures, news articles, slide shows, magazine articles, and their traditional communication with local media and the hunter and angler community. Then, under the Information Bureau's leader Steve Bayless, they found enough human and financial resources to publish a special issue of the agency's magazine and produce a thirty-minute movie, *The Yellowstone Concerto*. Both of these efforts, aimed exclusively at the preservation of the river, may well have been the most critical tactical steps in the campaign.

The magazine and movie were released after the hearings and before the board had to make its decision on the river's allocation. The application for the in-stream flow reservation was filed in November, 1976. The hearings were held in the summer of 1977. The special issue of the department's magazine, *Montana Outdoors*, was a comprehensive review of the river's history and ecology, and it addressed the full dimension of the decision at hand. It also revealed the emotional attachment that had grown among the biologists and others who had just spent four or five years of their lives in the river's presence. *The Yellowstone Concerto*, both visually and in narration, was an unabashed emotional appeal on behalf of the river. Both won national awards of recognition. The agency information officers were showing the movie in local theaters, public meetings, and through local television stations.

The Board of Natural Resources and Conservation contemplated the vast body of assembled information and struggled with decision deadlines and extensions. The net affect turned out to be a firm deadline by the end of December 1978. It was roughly a two year period from the application deadline in November of 1976 to an allocation of the Yellowstone River's future in late 1978. In that time we continued our full-throated advocacy for the river and kept in close association with non-government advocacy groups that joined us in the campaign. This struggle was biological, social, and political, a genuine three-ring circus. Then the phone rang.

Massachusetts, Kentucky, and New York Show Up

While we were focused on the critical public education component, I received a call from Tom Pero, the Massachusetts editor of *Trout Magazine,* the official publication of Trout Unlimited (TU). The editor was well aware that their Montana office and their local chapters here were actively involved in the struggle for the river. Pero had an idea that he thought might help and wanted my reaction and perspective. He had learned that Glenmore Distilleries, a Kentucky bourbon company, was about to introduce a new product called Yellowstone Mellow Mash. In that industry, the normal practice for introducing a new product was to sponsor a golf or tennis tournament. Tom's idea was to suggest they sponsor a campaign to call attention to the Yellowstone River, its peril and possible salvation.

The immediate response was "great idea" with some almost immediate but minor caveats relative to what was written and that a temperate tone be maintained. Tom then contacted Glenmore while we made sure a copy of our Yellowstone edition of *Montana Outdoors* and the movie *The Yellowstone Concerto* showed up on the desk of Fred Burghard Jr., vice president of Glenmore. In no time they pledged $50,000 to a national public information campaign. After a few telephone conversations with Glenmore and a contract relative to what was acceptable in news releases and other documents, we were under way. Sparks would fly.

Glenmore Distilleries hired Rand Public Relations of New York City to create a national awareness of the river and its peril. Their plan quickly included purchase of 30 copies of *The Yellowstone Concerto,* a national press tour, and when Yellowstone Mellow Mash went on sale, leaflets would be available urging tax-deductible contributions to the campaign. Those contributions were directed to the Joe Brooks Foundation in Livingston, Montana. Joe was a classic conservation-oriented trout fisherman, and the foundation's purpose was the preservation of the river he loved. The foundation was chaired by John Bailey, the second generation of the Dan Bailey Fly Shop family to introduce anglers to the Yellowstone and defend the river time and time again.

When Rand Public Relations called to discuss a national press tour, I had one stipulation: the tour must be held on or after the autumn equinox. The hope was that the Absaroka Mountains would have their first dusting of snow and the cottonwood trees along the river in Paradise Valley would be golden with autumn color. As it turned out, God and The Force were still with us; fresh snow and golden cottonwoods were on schedule.

Meanwhile at the political level, the incumbent governor, Tom Judge, won re-election, and he appointed an academic from the University of Montana's School of Forestry as the Fish and Game Director, the agency's first political appointee with limited fish and game experience. He also appointed a new Fish and Game Commission Chairman. If the intent of the changes was to temper our advocacy, the changes were too little, too late. The course we were on had a momentum of its own.

On September 18, 1978, Rand Public Relations landed in Helena to finalize the itinerary for the press tour. Closer to the river, John Bailey and river guide Ray Hurley were lining up fishing guides who volunteered to give the reporters a float on the river. Three days later we all assembled in Billings to welcome reporters from *Life, Omni, Audubon,* the *Wall Street Journal, Fly Fishing the West, Mariah, Trout, Outdoor Life, National Geographic, Business Week,* and a few others, even *Penthouse.* The tour got underway on September 21st with breakfast and a briefing at a local hotel. The briefing included a screening of *The Yellowstone Concerto.* Montana's lieutenant governor, Ted Schwinden, welcomed the reporters and suggested they also talk to other interest groups who wanted a piece of the Yellowstone River.

Later that morning, for the purpose of perspective, writers were flown in small aircraft over the coal fields, the two existing power plants out on the coal fields, and Yellowtail Dam on the Bighorn River. The planes then landed in Livingston where four station wagons hauled them to Chico Hot Springs Resort on the upper Yellowstone. "Camp" consisted of the fabled hot springs, a classic western saloon, and gourmet dining. That evening the hydrologists and the full team of biologists gave them the story. The next day, the volunteer fishing guides gave each writer ten miles of Yellowstone River trout fishing through Paradise Valley. It was September 22, there was fresh snow on the surrounding Absaroka peaks, and the cottonwood leaves were golden. We were a week and three months out from the December 1978 decision deadline.

Among the reporters was Joan Roesgen of the *Billings Gazette*. Her objective, at least in part, was to tell the Montana people what was going on. Her story was comprehensive, accurate, and dramatically presented on a page and half of the *Gazette's* Sunday edition. In a curious coincidence of timing, that Sunday was October 1, the opening day of the goose hunting season. Among those in the field was Montana Governor Tom Judge, hunting with the Fish and Game Commission chairman and the department's relatively new director, among others.

Following the morning hunt, the governor and others gathered for breakfast in the dining room of a Malta hotel. Lying in front of the governor's plate was the *Billings Gazette*. The breakfast was informal and various members of the hunting party took different sections of the *Gazette*. It wasn't long before all that was left in front of the governor was a section titled "Perspective." The Yellowstone story covered the entire front page plus a good bit of the next page. It included a map of the Yellowstone River on which sat a bottle labeled "Yellowstone 86 Proof...Aged 6 Years." That bourbon went into the Kentucky aging barrel in 1972, the same year we sent those three biologists into Paradise Valley to prevent Allenspur Dam.

The bold headline over Joan Roesgen's article read, "The selling of the Yellowstone...How Madison Avenue came to Montana...and launched a media blitz." Prior to becoming governor, Judge was professionally engaged in public relations. He knew instantly the potential impact of what he was learning about for the first time. I was told that as he read the story he repeatedly muttered "that son of a bitch." As he read, he turned to the Commission chairman and asked, "Did you know that s.o.b. was doing this?" The chairman nodded that he knew. The governor read some more and then turned to his relatively new director, Dr. Robert Wambach, with the same question and received the same answer. We were three months out from a decision.

Ten days after the governor's goose hunt, the results of the press tour started showing up. In the lead was a story in the *Wall Street Journal* delivered on October 11 under the headline, "Vast Deposit of Coal Fires Controversy Over Montana River." After that, nearly all the tour-produced articles favored the river. The only journal that did not publish anything was *Penthouse*. Apparently they found a reason to avoid the naked truth about the river's peril. The rest of the writers produced wonderful material that without exception portrayed the Yellowstone River as a treasure worth fighting for. The big score came just weeks before the Board

Jim at the North Fork of the Flathead *(Photo by John Frederick)*

had to make its decision. *Life* magazine gave "Great River in Crisis" ten pages in full color. That indeed was still another golden moment in the effort to preserve the treasured river. In a curious alignment of events through time, the first issue of *Life* magazine, published in November 1936, featured the building of Fort Peck Dam in Montana, the first of a series of dams that harnessed the wild Missouri River.

Most of the articles coming out of the press tour made note of the competence and dedication of those working to preserve the river. There was one article, however, that described us as we all wanted to see ourselves. Writing in the

December 1978 issue of *Fly Fishing the West*, reporter Don Roberts wrote:

> I had finally found a place where the agency people did not speak in tongues, did not hide behind jargon, did not hesitate to speak directly to the issue. In Montana the state wildlife people are real...you scratch them and they bleed (they will also claw back), show them a fish or a naked broad and they pant, fill their river with concrete and they cry.

That is who we wanted to be, and Don Roberts helped us believe that is who we were.

In late December 1978, the Montana Board of Natural Resource and Conservation made its decision. The Montana Fish and Game Department was granted an in-stream flow of 5.5 million acre feet, the largest in-stream flow for fish and wildlife in Montana history, and perhaps in U.S. history. We had asked for 8.2 million, but the 5.5 million allocation included seasonal high flows essential to maintaining a meandering river, which tactically at least precluded an impoundment on the main river, specifically Allenspur Dam. After the board's decision, the North Central Power Study faded, the Montana Wyoming Aqueduct Plan vanished, the projected twenty-some Montana coal-fired power plants ended up being four, and the Montana Power Company successfully lobbied the Legislature to become a de-regulated utility so it could transform into a high-tech communications company—and promptly collapsed.

The Yellowstone River is still 670 awesome miles of free-flowing river. Those of us who stood by her in the 1970s can now turn in at night with a little grin on our faces—

after at least one toddy of Yellowstone Mellow Mash Kentucky bourbon.

A Couple of Personal Fish Stories

On the personal side, while all of this river conservation activity was going on, my family of young sons was passing through their baseball playing years. That usually included the selection of Little League "All Star" teams and tournaments. For our family, that often meant days of multiple games played in Butte. On one occasion, between games, I took a walk along a stream that ran adjacent to the baseball complex. I encountered a couple of Butte youngsters fishing. I was aware of the fact that "Super Fund" resources had been reclaiming local streams after a century of mining pollution. The boys had a few trout on a stringer and I asked one of them, "What is the name of this stream?" The young Butte boy's response was, "I don't know, we call it shit creek. We don't eat these fish, we give 'em to the cat." Apparently stream restoration still had a ways to go.

On another occasion between games, I jumped in my car and drove to the nearest fishing access site on the Big Hole River. It was a few years after the Fish and Game Department had instituted Wild Trout Management and had stopped planting hatchery fish where natural reproduction was viable. It wasn't long before I caught and released a beautiful, one and a half pound, wild rainbow trout. I was alone, not another angler in site, and I thought of the battle fisheries biologists Dick Vincent and Ron Marcoux fought to make the switch from hatchery fish to wild trout management. I also vividly remembered the Fish and Game Commission meeting where the Fisheries Division Chief, Art Whitney, proposed switching to wild trout management. A skeptical commissioner asked

Art if he would resign if what he was proposing did not work. Art, without hesitation, answered in the affirmative. I had just experienced the net effect of those actions and years of habitat preservation. I knew why that fish was there. It was a special moment and not knowing what to do about it, I simply tucked my fly rod under my arm while I stood in mid-river and put my hands together, applauding the time, the place, and the fish. It was probably good that I stood there alone.

Goats, Grizzlies, and Gas on the Front

With each new generation, the human passion to "develop" or "exploit" a seemingly empty wild place springs anew. It is simply the nature of humans. Thus, as the 1970s came to a close, we moved the human and financial resources of the Ecological Services Division from the Yellowstone River to the Rocky Mountain Front (the Front). We also brought our operating style of soliciting funds from those wanting access to places we felt important to protect. As a result, we were able to field ecological studies aimed at grizzly bears, mountain goats, elk, bighorn sheep, mule deer, and raptors. This effort was designed to evaluate and perhaps challenge the myriad leases and permit applications for oil and gas

Rocky Mountain Front *(Photo by Kristi DuBois)*

pending on private, federal, and state lands. We hoped to do this by bolstering a strong Fish, Wildlife and Parks body of information already gathered along the Front. (In 1979 the 46th Montana Legislature renamed the Fish and Game Department the Montana Department of Fish, Wildlife and Parks—MFWP.)

In addition to the three wilderness areas along and to the west of the Front, the federal land and mineral estate included wilderness study areas on Forest Service and Bureau of Land Management lands, as well as other federal lands used for a variety of activities. The state land holdings included school trust lands and three wildlife management areas. The private estate included properties where the landowners held the mineral rights and places where they did not.

The Political and Personal Setting

President Nixon's 1973 call for energy independence stimulated more than the coal industry on the lower Yellowstone. The oil and gas industry also heard the call and renewed their interest in leasing, exploring, and drilling on what they knew geologically as the "over-thrust belt," and we knew as the Rocky Mountain Front and the wild lands beyond.

At the state level, the governor who barely tolerated our campaign on the Yellowstone left office at the end of 1980. The election that year was won by Ted Schwinden, who had been lieutenant governor in the previous administration. President Ronald Reagan entered the White House in that same election. He appointed James G. Watt as Secretary of the Interior. Watt's mantra was relatively simple: "We will mine more, drill more, cut more timber."[10] Watt once addressed

---

[10] Wikiquote.org/wiki/James_G._Watt.

the Western Council of State Governments and spoke of a proposal "to sell 35 million acres of public land to help pay the national debt." He also advocated the rapid development of oil on the public lands. The news story noted: "Watt's remarks brought a standing ovation from approximately 300 western legislators and other state officials."[11]

Watt's corporate pep-talk was a bit overboard for Montana's conservation ethic held both at the grassroots and to some extent at the political level. A part of Watt's vision was to seismically explore the Rocky Mountain Front and the Bob Marshall Wilderness. The people labeled it "Bombing the Bob." At the time, U.S. Congressman Pat Williams addressed a Helena service club. When he was asked about the proposal to "Bomb the Bob," his exacts words were "Not on my watch they won't!" The club, composed of civic and business leaders, rose as one in a standing ovation! The Montana people were not ready to yield the conservation masterpiece we knew as the "Bob" and "The Front." The contrast evident on the political scene was a good indication of the intensity of the battle at hand.

Pat Williams, a staunch, straight-forward conservationist, was one of two Montana congressmen at the time. Congressman Jim Battin had already stood up for conservation at a critical moment in this saga. In time, U.S. Senator Jon Tester would likewise take a hand in protecting the Front with the Rocky Mountain Front Heritage Act.

On the personal side, through the 1970s our family of six sons started becoming old enough to join the local Boy Scouts of America program. Their first Scout Master was John Grove, a close neighbor and forester employed by the U.S. Forest Service. The local troop's main summer event was a week-

[11] *Great Falls Tribune* (AP). "Watt reiterates need for development." August 26, 1982.

Jim and his sons, Eric and Brian coming out of the Scapegoat Wilderness.

long backpack trip, usually into a Montana wilderness area. Parents were invited to participate and a very few did. I was one of them. Our oldest son, Eric, convinced the family that this was something between a really good idea and an absolute necessity. Deferring to his leadership, backpacking led to a total family activity. Through the 1970s and mid-1980s, we visited the preserved backcountry from Glacier National Park to the northern borders of Yellowstone. This in turn produced a growing appreciation for nature and the values embedded in the very idea of wild land preservation. Those concepts and experiences quickly penetrated the way I addressed natural resource management issues on the job and through active participation in non-government conservation organizations. At times, my involvement with citizen conservation groups, while holding a government position, was criticized as a "conflict of interest." Since I worked for Fish, Wildlife and Parks, I chose to see it as a *"consistency of interest."*

94

Taking our Turn on the Front

As the Yellowstone battle was coming to a close, we were again reorganized. The Environment and Information Division became the Ecological Services Division. Gone was the direct tie between our field ecologists and the agency's communication/education capacity. January 1981 greeted us with a new governor, Ted Schwinden, a new Fish, Wildlife and Parks Commission, and a new department director, Jim Flynn.

There should have been more time to celebrate and reflect upon what worked on the Yellowstone stream-flow reservation campaign. However, the Rocky Mountain Front was already being hounded by the oil and gas industry. It didn't take long to decide where we might be of some use, so we took our people, our resources, and our tactics, and headed for the Front. We never put down the lance or took off our helmets. The Front would be the focus of the unit.

Geographically, "The Front" lies west of Augusta, Choteau, and Browning, stretching from the east slope of Glacier National Park in the north to Highway 200 on the south. It is where the geology of the Northern Rockies collides with the Northern Great Plains in rather dramatic style. To the east lay the sprawling northern plains, to the west lay our nation's most serious effort at preserving remnants of North America's wildness. Those efforts included a number of national forests and a significant portion of our society's desperate effort to cling to just a bit of wilderness. In this case, the designated wilderness areas were the Bob Marshall, the Scapegoat and the Great Bear.

The nurtured and now restored wildness of the Front included the state-owned Sun River, Blackleaf, and Ear Mountain wildlife management areas. In the private sector, wild land restoration and protection included The Nature Conservancy's Pine Butte Swamp, and then in 1987 the Boone and Crockett Club's Theodore Roosevelt Memorial Ranch was bought and dedicated. All these state and private properties were acquired by sportsmen and naturalists to facilitate an exceptional wildlife restoration process. The oil industry wanted leases, exploration permits, permits to drill, and pipeline corridors to figuratively suck up America's last wildest place and pump it away.

The state wildlife agency and central Montana sportsmen already had a long history of wildlife work along the Front. Our first step was to learn how those assets came through time to the current challenge. It gave us the necessary humility after the Yellowstone victory. More important, it gave us the perspective that we were a part of a conservation ethic buried generations deep in our Montana culture. Thus we began by trying to get in step with those who marched to the Front before us and then willed our generation the wildness we now sought to defend.

The Wild History of a Place

There are many descriptions of the wildlife abundance that Lewis and Clark observed as they navigated the Missouri River through the Northern Plains in 1805 and 1806. Captain Lewis left us a good taste on Monday, July 7, 1806. The Voyage of Discovery was returning eastward with Captain Lewis ascending the Big Blackfoot River. His component of the expedition crossed the Continental Divide over what is now called Lewis and Clark Pass. Lewis' diary notes on Tuesday July 8 that they "now felt, by the luxury of our food, that we were approaching once more the plains of the Missouri, so rich in game." Three days later they approached the vicinity of the Great Falls of the Missouri. The expedition recorded the following narrative:

> ...in the neighborhood the buffaloe (sic) are in such numbers, that on a moderate computation, there could not have been fewer than ten thousand within a circuit of two miles. At this season, they are bellowing in every direction, so as to form an almost continued roar, which at first alarmed our horses, who being from the west of the mountains, are unused to the noise and appearance of these animals.[12]

Eight decades later, a young Theodore Roosevelt published *Hunting Trips of a Ranchman and Wilderness Hunter* that told the story of a rancher looking for open range grazing opportunity on that same landscape. TR wrote:

> No sight is more common on the plains than that of a bleached buffalo skull; and their countless numbers attest the abundance of the animal at a time not so very long past...A ranchman who...had made a journey of a thousand miles across Northern Montana, along the Milk River, told me that, to use his own expression, during the whole distance he was never out of sight of a dead buffalo, and never in sight of a live one.[13]

That ranchman's journey was from near the North Dakota Border to within sight of the Rocky Mountain Front and back. Montana had become the wildlife boneyard of North America.

[12] Meriwether Lewis. *The Lewis and Clark Expedition Vol. 3*. J. B. Lippincott Co. Philadelphia and New York, 1961.
[13] Theodore Roosevelt. *Hunting Trips of a Ranchman & Wilderness Hunter*. Modern Library Edition, Random House, 1996.

The Road Back

Two years after that book was published, Roosevelt and associates formed the Boone and Crockett Club to introduce the sporting code to hunting and to begin the restoration of big game. Four years later, they amended our young nation's land disposal laws to allow presidents to set aside federal land as forest reserves. It was known as the "Creative Act."

On February 22, 1897, President Grover Cleveland designated the Lewis and Clark and Flathead Forest Reserves giving Montana wild lands and wildlife of the Rocky Mountain Front a reason to hope. When Theodore Roosevelt (TR) ascended to the Presidency, the "Creative Act" wound up in the hands of two of its creators, TR and Gifford Pinchot, "America's Forester." In their custody the forest reserves were consolidated into the National Forest system and expanded from about 40 million acres to over 190 million acres.[14] When he was done, TR told us:

> Westerners who live in the neighborhood of the forest preserves are the men who in the last resort will determine whether or not these preserves are to be permanent.[15]

In other words, for this to all work, there had to be a *Democracy of the Wild* and it had to be embraced, motivated, and ultimately expressed at the local grassroots level.

For the aspiration of America's conservation visionaries to become real, it would have to both 'touch the earth' and motivate the people in our evolving democracy. The truth-

[14] USFS Lands Staff. *Establishment and Modification of National Forest Boundaries and National Grasslands.* USDA FS 612, November 1997.
[15] Theodore Roosevelt. "Wilderness Reserves: The Yellowstone Park." *Outdoor Pastimes of an American Hunter.* Charles Scribner's Sons. 1905. pp. 320-353

of-history tells us that is exactly what happened. There was no better example than Montana's Rocky Mountain Front. While Montana had become a wildlife boneyard, the seed of a conservation ethic planted by people like James and Granville Stuart, sprouted. The restoration took time, but our conservation compass had an ethical heading.

Down on the Front

When the U.S. Forest Service was new, Ranger Elers Koch left the following account of wildlife populations on the Rocky Mountain Front and wild lands to the west:

> The South Fork of the Flathead and the Sun River country is today considered excellent game country. Deer, elk, and goats are relatively abundant, yet in the fall of 1905 and again in 1906 I rode for a month ... through the wildest part of that country with a rifle on my saddle, and with the exception of one goat never saw or got a shot at a single big game animal...[16]

This observation was made exactly 100 years after Captain Lewis' journal entry. At the time Theodore Roosevelt was our president and Gifford Pinchot was the head of the U.S. Forest Service. The Montana Fish and Game Department was less than ten years old, modestly funded, and focused on creating wildlife refuges, law enforcement, and fish hatchery production.

In 1913, seven years after Ranger Koch's ride, State Senator T. O. Larson of Choteau introduced "An Act to

[16] Koch, Elers. *Big Game in Montana from Early Historical Records.* The Journal of Wildlife Mgt. Vol. 4, No. 5, Oct. 1941.

Establish a Game Preserve in the Rocky Mountains, for the Protection of Game Animals and Birds." The Montana Senate passed the measure 26–0. The vote in the House was 62–2. This legislation created what was and remains today the Sun River Game Preserve on the South Fork of the Sun River. The national forest lands in the preserve would become wilderness when Congress passed the Wilderness Act in 1964, a half century plus one year later. Since protection of game animals within the preserve was absolute, even the grizzly bear picked up some de-facto protection more than 60 years before it was listed under provisions of the 1973 Endangered Species Act. In 1931, Montana made the grizzly bear a game animal so it could be protected and managed, and the Endangered Species Act was still 42 years off.

As Montana's "westerners" struggled with wildlife restoration, the nation was struck with the one-two-punch of the Great Depression and drought. To this day, the late 1920s and 1930s are remembered as our nation's "worst hard times." We were a country suffering through the economic collapse of the The Great Depression and the drought-driven environmental disaster of the Dust Bowl.

Author Timothy Egan tells us what it was like on the day of the worst dust storm of them all, Black Sunday, April 14, 1935, when "more than 300,000 tons of Great Plains Topsoil was airborne that day."[17] It dumped tons of soil on Chicago and darkened New York City and Washington, D.C.

The country was fortunate to have another Roosevelt in the saddle at this crucial time. From his perch in Washington D. C., President Franklin D. Roosevelt (FDR) observed:

---

[17] Egan, Timothy. *The Worst Hard Time.* A Mariner Book, Houghton Mifflin Company. Boston and New York, 2006

"There is a mysterious cycle in human events. To some generations much is given. Of other generations much is expected. This generation has a rendezvous with destiny."[18] Events about to occur in Washington D.C. would soon reach the Front.

In 1936, in the midst of the Great Depression and the Dust Bowl years, FDR convened the First North American Wildlife Conference. Hunters and anglers from across the nation, including seven from Montana, stood up and showed up. At that conference FDR challenged the attendees:

> It has long been my feeling that there has been lack of a full and complete public realization of our wildlife plight, of the urgency of it, and of the many social and economic values that wildlife has to our people. This and my firm belief in the ability of the American people...is what impelled me to call the North American Wildlife Conference.[19]

The people responded. They took a loose network of rod and gun clubs made up of local hunters and anglers, and forged a national force for conservation, the National Wildlife Federation. The Pittman-Robertson Act sailed through Congress the next year, going from introduction to the President's signature in 93 days! The act taxed firearms and ammunition and made the revenue available to the states for wildlife research and restoration. A great wildlife Renaissance was invigorated and those funds would soon reach the Front. The conservation ethic, introduced to a nation by TR, then

---

[18] Franklin D. Roosevelt. 1936. Taken from Howe presentation at the NSSF Summit, 2008
[19] Franklin D. Roosevelt. *Proceedings of the North American Wildlife Conference.* February 3-7, 1936

energized during the administration of FDR, grew strong in the people.

Idealism Funded

Early in the 20th century, the wildlife recovery debate along the Rocky Mountain Front was sharply focused on the competition between wildlife and livestock. Petitions to remove livestock from critical areas were advanced as were counter petitions favoring livestock production. Since the Office of State Game Warden was considered "unstable" and the state still lacked professional wildlife managers, the U.S. Forest Service was the target of the dueling parties.[20]

In 1940, the Forest Service designated a portion of Lewis and Clark National Forest as the Bob Marshall Wilderness, thus offering this unique wild place as much protection as it could within its regulatory authority. This was 24 years before Congress passed the Wilderness Act.

Early estimates of the number of elk remaining in the Sun River portion of the Rocky Mountain Front were highly variable, with the minimum estimate as low as 300 animals around 1910. Wildlife, however, was responding to the new protection offered. By 1917 the estimates for elk in the Sun River ranged from 1,708 to 5,000. As the tough times of the Great Depression and drought of the "Dirty Thirties" were endured, the competition between livestock and recovering wildlife became intense. A Great Falls sportsman and author wrote:

> In the Sun River…hard winters, lack of winter range drove the elk onto the ranches to invade haystacks

[20] Harold D. Picton and Irene Picton. *Saga of the Sun*. Montana Department of Fish and Game. 1975.

and livestock winter range;...but the ranchers had accepted it as one of the hazards of ranching in a big game area.[21]

In the classic Montana conservation tradition, the local people organized the "Sun River Conservation Council" to seek a solution. The group's conclusion would be to establish a winter range for elk. The recently enacted Pittman-Robertson Wildlife Restoration funds were the ultimate source of the funds. When this, one of the state's first acquisition efforts for wildlife, hit a crisis point, Choteau rancher Carl Malone and Great Falls hunter Tom Messelt put up their personal funds to hold the land and save the deal.[22] As a result, a rancher's land ethic and a hunter's wildlife conservation ethic made the Sun River Wildlife Management Area a reality. The Rocky Mountain Front was now a generation of Montanans beyond T. O. Larson's 1913 commitment that produced the Sun River Game Preserve on public land, and once again home to a growing abundance and diversity of wildlife.

As the years passed, other critical public and private habitats were protected and acquired. The Scapegoat Wilderness was created in 1972. Thanks to Cecil Garland of Lincoln and countless others, it was the first federal wilderness area created through the initiative of local people.

This particular battle began when the Forest Service unloaded a bulldozer at a road-end on the North Fork of the Blackfoot River. The dozer was to build a road up the North Fork and then down the Dearborn River, thus ecologically decapitating what was then known as the Lincoln Backcountry.

---

[21] Tom Messelt. *A Layman and Wildlife.* Montana Stationery Company, Great Falls, Montana 1971.

[22] Picton and Picton. *Saga of the Sun.* Montana Department of Fish and Game, 1975.

Cecil got word and called Montana Congressman Jim Battin.

Congressman Jim Battin called the Regional Forester and asked for thirty days to study the situation. The Congressman was told "you don't have thirty days." To which he responded, "I DAMN WELL BETTER HAVE THIRTY DAYS!" The Congressman got his 30 days, plans to log and road the Lincoln Backcountry faded, and Cecil Garland and associates eventually got the land into the wilderness system. In the hearing process, Cecil's testimony before Congress was sheer poetry. The power and beauty of his words moved everyone. In time three people who either were or would be the Montana governor spoke in favor of protecting this wild place: Tim Babcock (R), Forrest Anderson (D) and Tom Judge (D).[23]

While all this was going on I happened to be on one of my Boy Scout wilderness backpacking adventures. We began hiking at the trailhead on the North Fork of the Blackfoot, probably close to where that bulldozer once sat. On that trip Scout Master John Grove and I took the troop to the summit of Scapegoat Mountain. Around evening campfires I told the boys about Cecil and the Congressman. Upon leaving wild country, scouts always need milkshakes and we stopped in Lincoln to meet the need. While in the café I looked out the window and saw Cecil walking from his store to his home. Quickly hustling all the boys out of the café and halting Cecil, I then with considerable fan-fare said, "Boys – this is Cecil Garland!" The chattering youths fell dead silent—not a word, sound, or peep out of any of them. On the bus home I asked one of my sons, "Why didn't you guys say anything when I introduced Cecil?" My son's response was, "Dad, we all thought that to be in one of your stories like that—he had to be dead."

[23] Subcommittee on Public Lands; Committee on Interior and Insular Affairs United States Senate, on S1121, September 23, 1968

Although recently deceased, Cecil Garland was in the first group of individuals to be inducted into the Montana Outdoor Hall of Fame in 2014. In 1978, with the help of U.S. Senator Lee Metcalf, the Great Bear Wilderness was added to that wild place. Senator Metcalf was also inducted into the Montana Outdoor Hall of Fame in 2014.

As the various designations placed a growing protective mantle around federal land, the state stayed active acquiring the Ear Mountain and Blackleaf wildlife management areas on the Front. The Nature Conservancy joined the effort through the acquisition of the Pine Butte Swamp Preserve. When the Boone and Crockett Club approached its 100th anniversary, they invited various states to propose a conservation challenge worthy of their centennial year. In response, I drafted Montana's proposal for an acquisition along the Front. Montana won, and in 1987, the Boone and Crockett Club selected a site on the Front and honored the spirit of their founders with the acquisition of the Theodore Roosevelt Memorial Ranch. The ranch quickly became home to virtually all the species of wildlife that roamed there in pre-settlement years except the buffalo.

Contributing a Page to the Front's History

Fish, Wildlife and Parks had a strong wildlife data base essential for the management and restoration of wildlife resources. As a result, we were able to field additional ecological studies aimed at assessing risks that oil and gas development imposed on grizzly bears, mountain goats, elk, bighorn sheep, mule deer, and raptors.

We soon became part of the Rocky Mountain Front Interagency Task Force with the U.S. Forest Service, Bureau of Land Management, and U.S. Fish and Wildlife Service.

Some funding was secured from all of them along with contributions solicited from Superior Oil, ARCO, American Petrofina, Marcellus Merrill Engineering, Shell Western, Sun Exploration and Production, and a few others. Our appeal was straight-forward: they needed information to comply with growing environmental requirements and sensitivity. We were in a position to gather it and objectively interpret how wildlife responds to their activities.

Within the Ecological Services Division, the wildlife staff selections and administration was handled by Bob Martinka. Bob was skilled in finding and hiring the best qualified biologists for our various job contracts. Thus, the 1980s' line-up became Keith Aune and Tom Stivers on grizzly bears; Gayle Joslin, who had previous field experience on grizzlies and mountain goats, took on the goat research and wildlife management area environmental assessment work; Helga Ihsle worked on mule deer and helped on the goat and raptor work; Dan Hook focused on bighorn sheep and elk; while Kristi DuBois studied raptors. The contract work was coordinated with MFWP wildlife biologists Gary Olson and John McCarthy. The field work was augmented by Tim Andryk, a graduate student focused on bighorn sheep. These contract-supported studies produced scientifically sound information critical to protect the recovering wildlife of the Front.

Bob's biologist selection produced an equitable gender balance that was quite atypical in the wildlife profession in that era. In time, I came to think of those girls as the "Eighties Ladies." There is a song of that title and in the song there is a line to the effect that, "there ain't nothin' these ladies ain't tried." I know that the ladies on our Rocky Mountain Front team had snared grizzly bears and I was with two of them one

Jim, and Gayle Joslin at mountain goat trapping site. *(Photo by Helga Ihsle Pac)*

day when they fired a cannon net over an old salt-lick and captured seven mountain goats in a single shot! That was quite a rodeo and way more exciting than another line in that same old tune noting they "burned their candles at both ends."

The biologist selection process was probably influenced at a public meeting that involved grizzly bear biology that Bob had attended some years prior to the action on the Front. During that meeting, Gayle Joslin, who had been snaring, collaring, and tracking grizzlies on the U.S.-Canadian border, got into a lively debate with a person of a differing opinion. After the meeting, Bob asked Gayle if she enjoyed fighting in defense of wildlife. Gayle answered that she did. Bob's said, "Come see me about a job." The job was a mountain goat study as part of evaluating a proposed mine in the Cabinet Mountains.

As the Cabinet Mountains project was near completion, Gayle moved to the Front to study mountain goats and write environmental analysis of industry proposals to lease the Sun River Wildlife Management Area (WMA) and another company's plan to drill test wells on the Blackleaf WMA. Fish, Wildlife and Parks owned the surface of the Blackleaf but did not own the mineral estate. We were now dealing face to face with one company, Williams Exploration, that had selected a site on the Blackleaf WMA for a test well. As surface owners of the place, we prescribed an access route that would have the least impact on the WMA and the animals living there.

On March 26, 1981, I met with the local representative of Williams Exploration in Choteau to discuss access options to their selected drill site. Also present was Nels Thoreson, the Regional Supervisor of Fish, Wildlife and Parks, and several of his staff. None of us knew that at that very moment, a Williams contractor was already on the WMA with a bulldozer, cutting a road on the route the company wanted. Shortly after our meeting ended, we were discussing MFWP's next step when the telephone rang.

Gayle Joslin was on the phone. Having just moved to the project, she had been doing some reconnaissance on the Blackleaf where she encountered the bulldozer in operation. The dozer was cutting a new road across critical elk winter range. Tucking a tape recorder under her down jacket, Joslin confronted the dozer and its operator. After an exchange of words and opinions that was recorded over the noise of the idling bulldozer, they parted company. The operator was unwilling to stop his activity or identify himself. Gayle went to the nearest ranch house, found a telephone, and called us. I asked Gayle if she had a camera. When she affirmed that

The bulldozer in the Blackfeaf Wildlife Management Area, 1981.
(Photo by Gayle Joslin)

she did, I said, "Go back up there and shoot the hell out of 'em!" I then jumped into my car and headed to Helena. She captured some dramatic images that soon hit the pages of the *Great Falls Tribune.*

When reaching Augusta on the way back to Helena, I found a phone and made two calls that just could not wait. The first was to our relatively new director. He was a political appointee with no fish and wildlife experience. At the time he was in his third month at the helm. It took me some time to convince him that we had been violated and that I had to immediately call the *Great Falls Tribune* and let them know. After assuring him that we had Gayle's confrontation with the bulldozer on tape and she was taking pictures as we spoke, he agreed to my calling the *Tribune.* I might have even told him that this gash across the face of the Front would be visible from Bynum.

The next call was to Bert Lindler, outdoor reporter for the *Tribune*. The fight was soon out in the open and we were clearly and publically in the position of defending the wildlife conservation legacy of the Rocky Mountain Front. We were not a silent bystander content to measure the loss. On the Blackleaf, the conflict had just begun.

Negotiating the terms of access to the Blackleaf became a lengthy and adversarial process. The Montana Oil and Gas Conservation Commission (MOGCC) was the permitting agency, Williams Exploration was the applicant, and MFWP was the land surface owner. As the negotiations between MFWP and Williams continued relative to where to put the access road, well site, and pipeline corridor, we realized there had been no compliance with the Montana Environmental Policy Act (MEPA) when the permit to drill was issued. We then learned that the MOGCC had not ever done any MEPA compliance associated with their permitting process, nor were they anxious to do so. In addition, reclamation of the road cut through the elk winter range was now part of the conversation.

The MFWP legal staff researched the issue, concluded a case could be made that the MOGCC needed to comply with MEPA, and prepared a challenge. To do so required that we give notice of our intent to take legal action if necessary and such a notice was filed. Word of our intent quickly circulated. Suddenly our negotiations with Williams Exploration took on a whole new tone. The company's insistence that they had rights as a mineral estate holder switched to a willingness to accept anything that we might suggest. We suspected that Williams' colleagues in the exploration industry and/or the MOGCC influenced their conservation epiphany. They were not anxious to start complying with MEPA.

The outcome of this particular confrontation was full reclamation of the road dozed through the southeast facing slope needed by wintering elk. A less disruptive access alignment was accommodated to the well site. A well was drilled and a pipe buried to move their product to a collection facility located off the wildlife area. A year or so later, the Fish and Game Commission asked for a report on the outcome of the access road and pipeline corridor restoration. I returned to the site with a video camera and crew. Before going afield the local grizzly bear manager was consulted. It was late spring and we learned the Blackleaf WMA was one of the sites used for dead livestock disposal.

We approached the pipeline reclamation site in a manner that gave us a good view of the area from a distance. We observed a sow grizzly and two cubs feeding on one of the disposed cattle carcasses. While filming the scene through telescopic lenses, I placed a blade of grass between my thumbs and blew it like a high pitched whistle. It produced a sound not unlike those made by calf elk. Not long afterward the sow grizzly and her cubs casually drifted our way. After they entered some heavy cover just below us, we decided to retreat to the safety of our truck, leaving the running video camera on the tripod. The last image on the video is the sow emerging from the heavy cover, standing at the base of the tripod, and issuing an audible *"woof"* to her cubs before running off across the foothills of the Blackleaf. We concluded that if the pipeline reclamation was found suitable to mother grizzly, it was acceptable to Montana Fish, Wildlife and Parks.

Given our experience on the Blackleaf, there was considerable reluctance to the idea of letting the oil and gas industry on the Sun River WMA. The environmental assessment Gayle Joslin wrote in consideration of that option concluded that if leases were granted, they would have to be done on a "no surface occupancy" basis. That recommendation prevailed. The Ecological Services Division, however, was not destined to prevail.

Ecological Services
Bites the Dust

We trained hard, but it seemed that every time we were beginning to form up into teams we would be reorganized. I was to learn later in life that we tend to meet any new situation by reorganizing—and a wonderful method it can be for creating the illusion of progress while producing confusion, inefficiency, and demoralization.

Petronius, A.D. 27-66

It was 8:15 a.m. on December 12, 1982, and I was at my desk as the head of the Ecological Services Division. At that point, Jim Flynn, the director of Fish, Wildlife and Parks, informed me that he and I were meeting with Governor Schwinden at 11 a.m. The state legislature was scheduled to convene next month, and state agencies had prepared budgets to allocate their resources for the two-year period beginning in July 1983. Rumors of an intent to eliminate the Ecological Services Division were widely known within state government and in the citizen conservation community. The budget prepared by Fish, Wildlife and Parks had dispersed the division's projects into other parts of the department. The citizens were starting to express themselves.

When we arrived at the governor's office, I was surprised to find my friend Phil Tawney in the room. I had no better friend than Phil. We met in 1971 when he and his wife Robin spent the winter in Helena while Phil worked as a University of Montana (UM) legislative intern and Robin worked on her senior paper for the UM School of Journalism. The following legislative session in 1973, they teamed up with Don Aldrich, the executive director of the Montana Wildlife Federation, to form the Environmental Lobby. After the session, the Tawneys moved from Missoula to Helena and, with the help of many others, founded the Montana Environmental Information Center (MEIC).

We became close friends, hunting buddies, handball opponents, and partners on a variety of conservation crusades. One night Phil was traveling out of town when Robin realized that their first born was ready to arrive ahead of schedule. Robin called for a ride to the hospital. Since Robin knew I was the father of six sons, she correctly assumed I knew where the hospital was. The result was the first child in the Phil and Robin Tawney family, a son they named Land.

Phil had a rich history of political and environmental activism. In addition to the Environmental Lobby and MEIC, he had founded the Montana Committee for an Effective Legislature (MontCEL) and also served as executive secretary of the Montana Democratic Party. At the time of this meeting, he was back in Missoula attending the UM School of Law.

I had no idea Phil was going to be there, and to this day I don't know how he knew what was about to transpire. I can only suspect the governor was starting to hear from his constituents on the matter of eliminating Ecological Services and was becoming a bit irritated by it all and suspected Phil had a hand in the unrest at the grassroots. The meeting started promptly and without the usual pleasantries that often initiate gatherings of people who have known each other for a while. I remember with some clarity the first words out of the governor. They were: "Phil, you have got a firestorm going on out there and I want to see it stopped!" To which Phil replied,

"Governor, I haven't lifted a finger yet, but if you want to see a firestorm I will show you one!" That was the opening salvo.

During the course of the discussion, Phil expressed both disagreement with the proposal to break up the Ecological Services Division and a general dissatisfaction with the governor's lack of communication with the conservation community. He also made the point that he and others of his persuasion believed in and had supported the governor, and now simply felt bad at what they perceived as a lack of consideration of their feelings and values. The governor responded by expressing his satisfaction in the job the director was doing and a perceived improved public image of the Department of Fish, Wildlife and Parks.

Throughout the wide ranging interchange of perspectives, the governor repeatedly pointed out the need to "take the lightning rod down," usually followed by the qualifier to retain the agency's work on the issues. At the time, I took the "lightning rod" to be me. In response, Phil stressed the concern went beyond the individual and went to "the heart of the department's ability and willingness to effectively deal with fish and wildlife habitat preservation efforts." Both the governor and director made general reference to using my redirected efforts to getting the entire department more directly involved in the habitat preservation agenda. At one point the governor challenged me to strive for this expanded goal. Both the governor and director stated several times they were, "not out to get anyone and if they were, there were better ways of doing that." This reminder was not presented in a threatening manner, and usually included reference to the promise that I would be given "meaningful work."

On three separate occasions the governor posed the question, "What would it take to satisfy the conservation

Ecological Services Division
Left to Right: Glenn Phillips, Bill Gardner, Bob Martinka, Fred Nelson, Gary Dusek, Larry Peterman, Kerry Constan, Dan Hook, Ron Stoneberg, Susan Curley, Jim Posewitz, Heidi Youmans, Serena Andrew, Dick Munro, Kristie DuBois, Rod Berg, Ralph Boland, Steve Knapp, and Pete Martin. Team members not present for the photo include: Rich DeSimone, Gayle Joslin, Tom Stivers, Keith Aune, Tom Hinz, Bruce Rehwinkel, Mike Haddix, Christopher Estes, and Liter Spence. *(MFWP photo)*

community?" On the third occasion the governor asked Phil directly if he "would be satisfied if Poz called you in two weeks and said it was OK?" Phil responded that he would. The lesson I learned in those two hours was the importance of being one with the constituents you serve and whose values you represent. They were there. In one way or another they were all there on that day and the people of the Ecological Services Division were not "thrown under the bus."

There was a golden moment during that intense discussion. At one point the governor was expressing his exasperation with the public comment he was enduring. During a rather lengthy review of those commentaries, he mentioned only one name. He specifically took note of being contacted by Urana Clark. Ms. Clark was a retired elderly lady living on an island in the Yellowstone River near Livingston. During our seven-year campaign for the river, I went to her home to explain what we were doing. At that time, we had tea and she affirmed her strong approval and support for preserving a free-flowing river. Her support, her Montana conservation ethic, was still there and in that room on that day in December 1982.

The meeting ran an hour past its assigned time and finally broke up when the governor's secretary interrupted with notice of another scheduled appointment. Three days later, MFWP circulated a summary prepared by the Governor's Council on Management suggesting a number of changes in state government. They included #213. It was reorganizing Fish, Wildlife and Parks, "emphasizing planning, centralizing research and exercising more central control over regional activities." The organizational chart in that document contained no Ecological Services Division. A week later, on December 21, 1982, I assembled the people who were the Ecological Services Division and distributed a memo to each of them on the subject of "Reorganization." It follows:

Office Memorandum

To: The Eco Services Personnel
Date: 12/21/82
From: Jim Posewitz
Subject: Reorganization

By now all of you have heard that our division will be disbanded as part of department reorganization. There are some things I need to share with you.

Ever since the subject was open for discussion, we have participated fully. This was done in verbal debate and in writing. In essence, no opportunity to argue our position was ignored. If you are interested, the written material can be made available.

On December 16, the director told me he had made his decision and received approval for his proposal from the management team working with the governor's office. That decision terminated Eco Services - probably effective June 30, 1983.

The director assured me that none of the functions and none of the people would be terminated. If savings are possible, they will be achieved in time and through attrition.

In response, I informed the director that it has always been my personal philosophy to support the director and his decisions as long as I worked for the organization. I do not intend to depart from that course.

Believe me when I say that I am aware of the anger and frustration many of you feel - I share it. We must not let those emotions govern our actions. We have been in existence in one form or another since 1969. In that time we survived numerous challenges to our work, our methods, and our existence.

Through that time and the opportunities it presented, we were propelled by hope, determination and pride. We must not tarnish our record or dim our achievements by finishing our race with either grief or regret.

We had our years in the sun and wasted none of them. I am content to let history judge us; let there be not one sour note in our concerto.

I expect each of you to spend the next six months working with the same vigor and determination you showed on the day you started. Each day is precious - treat it as such. When we hit the end of the chain, let it be at full throttle. Carry that momentum to your new assignments and make it contagious. Above all, be proud of what you have already accomplished. I know of no organization in or out of government that can match your record of achievement.

Some time in the spring—the season of new life—we will gather once more to lift a beer and shed a tear in celebration of one hell of an outfit.

Following the December 21st meeting, it took only two days before the Montana press corps was taking notice of the administration's intent. It began with a December 23 story in the *Great Falls Tribune*. From that point through the end of the year the *Helena Independent Record*, the *Missoulian*, the *Butte Montana Standard* and the *Livingston Enterprise* all chose to editorialize and comment in defense of the Ecological Services Division. Their attention persisted into January 1983.

I wrote several memos during that period to both communicate my point of view and to create a written record of what was going on. Three of those memos were written in long-hand, either as records for the file or for distribution to individuals. The intent was to skip the secretarial step to avoid stimulating the rumors already in circulation. The content of two of those memos, both written on January 5, 1983, follows:

To: File
Date: 5 January 1983
From: Poz

Subject: Reorganization

At 1:30 PM on 5 Jan. 1983 Director Flynn called Marcoux and me to his office. He was obviously enraged with the primary source of that irritation being a Great Falls Tribune story[24] on stream access of January 2, 1983. Further fueling his rage was the Livingston Enterprise editorial of December 29th, 1982, and the general reaction he is getting relative to his reorganization.

His primary point was that Marcoux and I had better come in with a plan to carry out his reorganization Friday and that I had better be prepared to tell the conservationists on Monday that it would work in no uncertain terms. He went on to say I had better make his reorganization work or I was "going down the road."

His main point was that he felt he was giving this organization as much as any man and all he was getting was abuse on himself and his family. During the course of the conversation he indicated several times that he may simply resign and has told the Governor he would have his decision by Monday morning.

---

[24]My original memo had the newspaper wrong. This correction identifying the *Great Falls Tribune* was made after former director Flynn reviewed a draft portion of text. September 13, 2017.

Marcoux and I said not a single word. It was obvious there was no room for discussion. In fact, when dismissed we were told it was not open for any discussion.

There was little doubt in my mind that the man was enraged. His voice would "break" on occasion, and his hands were shaking. We did nothing to further enrage him.During the course of the monolog names mentioned were Leonard Sargent, Phil Tawney, Mons Tiegen, Les Pengelly and perhaps a few others. Flynn's comment was we would all be better off if they were wiped from the face of the earth.   (Memo Complete 2:37 PM 5 Jan 83 Poz)

On the same day the above memo to the file was written, I wrote in longhand and hand-delivered the following memo to the Associate Director and the Deputy Director of Fish, Wildlife and Parks:

TO: Marcoux and Lewis 5 January '83
FROM: Poz
SUBJECT: Reorganization

Finally surfacing during our reorganization discussions are issues that are at the core of the idea to disband Ecological Services. They are issues that have been rumored enough around the Dept. that I'm sure the Director heard them from Dept. people. I hoped they weren't part of reorganization thinking but now I believe they probably were. I fear they left an impression on the Director that was not based on any truth.

Yesterday two of them were finally discussed, "duplication of effort" and "Eco Services goes off in its own direction." This being said however, no one present could offer one concrete example of either. When I pressed the question the answer was silence. Four people who collectively know more about what's going on in this Dept. could not supply one specific example of either of these widely held "beliefs." For 14 years Eco Services did what no one else was doing and in that time no one can give a single example of an agenda that did not have whatever authorization was needed from proper authority.

Every budget was reviewed and approved by Directors and Commissions. Every contract was approved by the Commission when that was appropriate and brought before them for information purposes when that was no longer necessary. For six years we have met every Monday with our superiors specifically to avoid overstepping our bounds. No other division has done that much less had the initiative to set it up.

I renew the challenge – give one specific example of either. Yet for years those charges were leveled & rumors passed and apparently believed. People who knew of no examples of either accepted them in quiet acquiescence. People who should have known better accepted them without challenge and thereby contributed to the myth. People who should have asked for specifics before passing judgment sat in silence.

What is being accomplished by all this is good men are being demeaned, discouraged and manipulated to design a system to solve a problem that never existed. There may be reasons for disbanding an organization

> with a respectable record of achievement. If so let's deal
> with valid reasons so reorganization can improve on our
> present flaws. If Eco Services must be buried let its eulogy
> contain the truth.

Over the next six months, virtually all the components and
projects of the Ecological Services Division were transferred
into either the Fisheries Division or the Wildlife Division. The
exceptions were Bob Martinka, a secretary, Serena Andrew,
and me. We became the Resource Assessment Unit attached
to the Director's office. At the time, most of the division's
resources were deployed addressing oil and gas developments
along the Rocky Mountain Front. While we were no longer
in the position of supervising those projects, we were in a
position in the director's office where on occasion we could
be helpful. Out in the field, the people stayed focused on the
wildlife and the land that sustained the remarkable wildlife
recovery that had occurred on their watch. In addition, they
stayed close to the grassroots residents of the Rocky Mountain
Front who, like the generation before them, carried the
Montana Wildlife Conservation ethic.

But Who Done It?

Fifteen years plus a few months later, the source of
the political "lightning" that struck the Ecological Services
Division still bothered my mind. In 2008, I was scheduled
to attend a conference in Phoenix and I knew that former
governor Schwinden, who had called the December 12,
1982, meeting, was retired there. We exchanged pleasant
correspondence and he agreed to meet with me. I was upfront

with my purpose, writing in my initial correspondence to him: "As I recall part of the conversation, it had to do with my having become a lightning rod and that had to be taken down. What I remain curious about was where the lightning was coming from."

Thus, the afternoon of March 24, 2008, found me knocking on a third-floor door of a condominium complex. The former governor's wife had passed on and he was living alone, looking out the window at a condo just like the one we were sitting in. Prior to entering politics, he had farmed and ranched in wide-open Roosevelt County, Montana, on America's Northern Great Plains. That condo setting still haunts me a bit. We spent a most pleasant afternoon together and what I learned was that he could not remember! It did bother me that two of the most vivid hours of my life were not all that important to a governor with dozens of issues of greater urgency. Then, eleven days later, he called.

The former governor left a message that he had a clue as to where the lightning came from. He said, "It was Bob Marks." Bob was a conservative Republican, long-time state legislator, and Speaker of the House. Along the way I learned the head of the Appropriations Committee wanted the Ecological Services Division removed from the budget. A progressive Democrat, Francis Bardenouve, known as the "conscience of the legislature," was said to have opposed that action but didn't have the votes to prevail. The net effect of it all was that Ecological Services got hacked in the budget process.

After wondering for years exactly where political pressure for taking down the Ecological Services Division came from, it remains a bit of a mystery. I was content to just be angry at those who carried the message to me. Now I am haunted by the idea that what the governor imposed was the only thing he could do to save the work and the people of the Ecological Services Division. By dispersing them, he could hide them and the resources they needed in the budgets of other divisions. As for the "lightning rod," I was kept in the agency for another decade, and as it turned out, there was a little spice in that as well.

As far as the search for the source of the "lightning" and exactly who put their sights on Ecological Services, I settled for a line in a song Bob Dylan wrote and I loved hearing Joan Baez sing in the 1960s. The song was "A Hard Rain's A-Gonna Fall," and the line was, *"And the executioner's face is always well hidden."*

A Personal Note

On a personal note, it was during this time that I sought and obtained dissolution of marriage that legally ended my marriage with Helen Vidal Posewitz. Five of the six sons born to that marriage were either through or about to enter college; the first born was deceased as the result of a motorcycle crash.

At the time of the dissolution, the boys were scattered from coast to coast and one was still living in Montana. The thirty-some years we spent together were richly endowed with outdoor adventures and a wide variety of shared experiences. Helen moved on to a variety of independent adventures and new life experiences of her own. I soon bonded with my present wife, Gayle Joslin, whose career and life ambitions were nearly identical to my own.

Back to the Front

While the administrators and politicians struggled to relocate the bureaucratic lightning rod, the field people of the Ecological Services Division remained focused on protecting the wildlife of the Rocky Mountain Front. They had been in the field since the later years of the 1970s, gathering detailed information and sharing it with the Montana people who knew and valued the wild lands. In the 1980s, it became more specific and intense.

Arco Oil and Gas Company applied for a prospecting permit from the South Fork of the Flathead to a point near the Swan River. Mile-Hi Exploration proposed using helicopters and a 20-man crew in the road less alpine country. Consolidated Georex Geophysics requested a permit to set off 5,400 dynamite charges over a 207-mile grid in the Bob Marshall, Scapegoat, and Great Bear wilderness country. While these and other applications to explore or lease portions of this wild-land complex were pending, the U.S. Forest Service leased the mineral rights on 42,000 acres in the Deep Creek Roadless Area. The action was appealed by growing citizen opposition but at the time it was supported by the Chief of the Forest Service.[25] The political environment at the federal level included President Ronald Reagan and Secretary of Interior James Watt. Before being appointed Secretary of Interior, Watt led the Mountain States Legal Foundation, a group known to intervene on behalf of the "drill baby drill" gas and oil industry. By 1982, the Lewis and Clark National

---

[25] *Great Falls Tribune,* "Forest Service chief upholds oil-gas leasing in roadless area." May 15, 1981.

Forest had put up every acre along the Front for lease, and the industry was gobbling them up. The conservation community took their advocacy to Congress in a Montana Wilderness Bill that would have extended wilderness protection to a variety of places, including areas of the Rocky Mountain Front. That legislative effort wound up on President Reagan's desk—where it died for lack of his signature.

As the political and environmental debates swirled, the citizens rallied. It wasn't long until one of them hung the moniker "Bombing the Bob" on the whole affair, and it took off like magic. In no time there arose the Flathead Committee to Save the Bob Marshall, the Bob Marshall Alliance, the Choteau-based Friends of the Rocky Mountain Front, and a focused commitment to the Front from the traditional state and national conservation groups. The three-word slogan said all that needed to be said. It had a power of its own. It is impossible to estimate the volume of written material and human energy that was invested in the battle. In the end, it boiled down to "Bombing the Bob vs. Drill Baby Drill." Nobody misunderstood what was being debated. Montana's elected officials from the state capital to the U.S. Congress immediately saw where this parade was headed, got out in front of it, and genuinely helped lead it consistent with that old and deep Montana Conservation Ethic that still runs through us.

In the field, the wildlife biologists of the Ecological Services Division were blended administratively into the Wildlife Division of Fish, Wildlife and Parks. As specific exploration activities were monitored, their effect on wildlife moved from speculative to measurable impacts. Those impacts included relocation of wildlife to marginal habitats and severe, measurable stress in some species, particularly mountain goats. For example, helicopter over-flights and associated aerial harassment caused mountain goat productivity to plummet, resulting in measurable population declines. As the factual base of the people's inherent conservation ethic was strengthened, so were their results. Law suits, appeals, and insistence on more sophisticated environmental analysis, held off or delayed on-the-ground activity.

While the citizens were exercising their legal options, the agencies that were focused on the Front cooperatively drafted and adopted "Management Guidelines for Selected Species – Rocky Mountain Front Studies" in 1987. Those studies were for the most part conducted by the now blended Ecological Services Division and Wildlife Division of Montana Department of Fish, Wildlife and Parks. The guidelines were science-based, designed to protect wildlife, and were basically institutionalized. There was some interagency friction as federal agencies tried to walk the tough line between their multiple-use objective and the "Interagency Rocky Mountain Front Guidelines." A major breakthrough came in 1997 when Lewis and Clark National Forest Supervisor Gloria Flora suspended mineral leasing on 356,000 acres. It was an action strengthened when the U.S. Senators from Montana, Max Baucus and Conrad Burns, legislatively made the suspension permanent in 2006.[26]

Although Gloria took decisive action in the 1990s, I tend to think of her as one of those Eighties Ladies who "burned their candles at both ends" along with Gayle, Helga, and Kristi of the former Ecological Services Division. Since I can't seem to forget those ladies, I suspect the Rocky Mountain Front and the wild places beyond also remember them, and will forever.

[26] *High Country News.* "Perseverance pays off for the Rocky Mountain Front." Gabe Furshong, Jan.1, 2015.

Persistent citizen participation, strengthened by reliable scientific information, put the brakes on "drill baby drill." The local people, many from the community and ranchlands west of Choteau, weren't finished. In response to their insistence, the entire Montana Congressional delegation helped draft and introduce protective federal legislation in October of 2011. That effort soon produced the "Rocky Mountain Front Heritage Act." When it came time to bring the whole thing across the finish line, U.S. Senator Jon Tester took a leadership role and delivered the legislation to the president's desk on or near December 12, 2014. Unlike the President Reagan veto of an earlier effort, this time the sitting president signed it into law on December 19, 2014. That president was Barack Obama.

While this entire environmental drama was unfolding, I was living in a home with a piano in the basement and a rather creative young man who could play it. The young man was Clayton J. DeSimone. His mother, Gayle Joslin, was one of the Front's Eighties Ladies. She was the wildlife biologist on the mountain goat project. She also wrote the environmental assessment for the Sun River Wildlife Management Area. Clayton happened to be working on an original, rather bold and dramatic musical composition. As young Clayton was pounding the keyboard in the basement, all his Mom and I could see in our minds and think of was the Rocky Mountain Front. With his permission, we named his creation, "Ode to the Rocky Mountain Front." In time, we had it recorded and Choteau game warden Dave Wedum created a DVD with images of the Front and its wildlife set to the music.

Some years later, soon after the Rocky Mountain Front Heritage Act was signed, the conservation community held a thank-you dinner for Senator Tester. The event was held in the grand banquet room of Helena's historic Montana Club. Through many years the elegant, richly paneled dining room hosted events sponsored and attended by Butte's "Copper Kings" and a passing parade of politicians, land barons, and dignitaries who fostered Montana's exploitive history. On this particular night, however, the room belonged to the people and a U.S. Senator who was their champion. The room had a piano.

When the senator entered the room, I waited for a chance to have a private word, gave him a DVD of the "Ode to the Rocky Mountain Front," and told him the young man playing the piano as background to the social gathering was young Clayton. I then asked if the Senator would like to hear the "Ode" if we could catch a private moment. This was done through the social chatter of a room packed with celebrators. The Senator listened with focused attention. Later, to my surprise, I learned the Senator, in addition to his ranching background, was trained in music and had taught the subject in the public school system. The Senator thanked Clayton and returned to the event at hand.

That evening included a list of conservation speakers thanking the Senator for the "Heritage Act" now protecting 275,000 additional acres of the Front, including 67,000 acres added to the Bob Marshall and Scapegoat wilderness areas. When they concluded, the Senator took the microphone for closing remarks. When he finished, he paused and then took note of a fifth-generation, young Montanan whose family homesteaded along the Front and remains dedicated to its preservation. He told the assembled that the young man had composed an original piece of music called "Ode to the Rocky Mountain Front," that he was present and had been entertaining them all evening. The Senator then suggested the assembled listen. He then invited Clayton back to the piano.

The room hushed, the silence was absolute. Clayton's fingers began whispering the awe-inspiring beauty of the landscape and built to a crescendo of power and glory inherent in wild country. He played to, and his every note was heard by, a room filled with people who knew the Front. The assembled had ranched its foothills, hunted its deepest wild places, teased its trout with flies and worms, nurtured its elk and deer, thrilled at the sight of mountain sheep and mountain goats, and chose to respect rather than challenge the grizzly's position in the food chain. When Clayton hit that last note, and dropped his hands into his lap, the room erupted. Every man, woman, and child rose to their feet. The thundering ovation that followed was deafening and protracted. For the Rocky Mountain Front it was indeed—a golden moment.

Cinnabar

In the days when the circus came to town, they often advertised that they came with "three rings." For me, the 1980s were like that. In the Center Ring was the nation's energy crisis. Ring Two was trying to hang on in an agency charged with protecting fish and wildlife. Ring Three contained citizen activists rallying to the defense of the environment. Activity in the Center Ring featured the federal government and energy corporations going after coal, oil, and water along with politicians dancing in a variety of directions. In Ring Two, my state government unit, designed for and experienced in habitat protection, was being politically dispersed. Ring Three featured the soul of America and our "democracy of the wild." That Ring held the growing non-government citizen conservation movement. In reality, these three rings were often linked and it was indeed a rare privilege to have had a hand and a foot in each. It was quite a circus! The Cinnabar Foundation was born, lived, and prospered in Ring Three.

The seven-year campaign to gain an in-stream flow allocation for the Yellowstone River saw numerous public meetings and hearings along the 670-mile course of the river. Generally, land owners and irrigators living on or near the headwaters opposed an in-stream allocation. Those living on the lower river tended to be a bit more sympathetic. There was an exception. There was one ranch owner who lived on a headwaters tributary of this last great river who consistently showed up at hearings, conferences, and informational meetings. He came to express support for protecting in-stream flows. It didn't take long to realize how exceptional that rancher really was.

It took Leonard Sargent a while to get to Montana, but we all should be glad he came. Born in Baltimore in 1912, Leonard's service began as the three-year-old son of Commander Leonard Rundlett Sargent who militarized and protected the Panama Canal through World War I. When his turn came in World War II, Leonard hunted and destroyed Nazi submarines in the Mediterranean and participated in a diversionary landing there to tie down axis forces during the D-Day invasion of Normandy.[27]

After the "Big War," Leonard returned to The Taft School in Watertown, Connecticut, where he spent a career teaching mathematics and science while also coaching tennis and hockey. His hockey teams were so dominant in western New England that in time Leonard's team labeled him the "Winter God."[28] Leonard spent his summers cruising the Rocky Mountain west in search of the perfect retirement spot. In 1962 he found it in at the head of Cinnabar Creek, a headwater tributary to the Yellowstone River near Yellowstone National Park, and bought a chunk of land big enough to ranch on. The purpose of ranching was to secure the water rights through continued use and also to retain the ranch's tenure on public land grazing options. The place became his summer get away until he thought he retired seven years later.

In 1969, Leonard moved to the ranch on a permanent basis, married a former sweetheart, Sandy Packard Hubbard, and the Cinnabar Ranch was anchored. In an interesting alignment, 1969 was also the year the Montana Fish and Game Department created the Environmental Resources Division. Inevitably our trails would cross. In retrospect, the

---

[27]Tawney Nichols, Robin. *Len and Sandy Sargent, A Legacy of Activist Philanthropy.* The University of Montana Press, Missoula, Montana, 2008.
[28] Ibid.

CINNABAR
FOUNDATION

Cinnabar Foundation logo

genesis of the Cinnabar Foundation mirrored a conservation reformation that occurred in Montana political action from 1969 through 1975. That reformation included improving almost all of Montana's natural resource management laws, including extending recognition and attention to fish and wildlife values. In 1972, a new State Constitution became part of the fundamental change that occurred. That document included the following language: "The state and each person shall maintain and improve a clean and healthful environment...." The year the new constitution was adopted was the same year I moved three fish and wildlife biologists into Paradise Valley of the Yellowstone to prepare for the river's defense.

The social and political momentum of that era generated a growing number of non-profit citizen conservation/environmental groups. Among them was the Montana Environmental Information Center (MEIC), founded by Phil and Robin Tawney in 1973. From the start, the Sargents were personally guiding and financially stabilizing that and other fledgling groups. Before long, MEIC was in full flight as Montana's leading environmental citizen advocacy organization. As expansion and growth in the private conservation advocacy movement blossomed, those seeking financial support found their way up the long dirt road that ended in Cinnabar Basin and the Sargent's front yard.

It did not take long for the Sargents to realize they needed a system or program to help evaluate the growing number of individuals and organizations seeking vital assistance. As a result, they decided to create the Cinnabar Foundation to bring a bit of order to the process and maybe cut down on the traffic on that long dirt road up to the head of Cinnabar Creek. On February 23, 1983, Leonard Sargent affixed his signature to the Cinnabar Foundation's Articles of Incorporation and brought the foundation to life. Leonard invited Phil Tawney and me to join him as founding board members.

This action occurred two months after the Montana governor directed that the Ecological Services Division of the Montana Department of Fish Wildlife and Parks be dispersed. It also occurred four months before that division's final biennial budget ran out, and it would disappear as a division within the agency. At the same time, by their actions if not their words, my friend Leonard and good buddy Phil were telling me there would always be room for me within the conservation movement and that they were looking out for me.

As originally constructed, the Cinnabar Foundation was designed to be a modest entity, and it would be endowed with assets from the sale of the ranch when the Sargents passed on. Our area of granting was defined as Montana and the Greater Yellowstone Ecosystem. In 1985, our three-person board met to make its first grants out of a relatively small amount of available funds. The two-hour board meeting that year was squeezed in around three days of elk hunting out of the ranch. We made two grants totaling $1,123. In short order, Leonard added a substantial amount of money to the

Len and Sandy Sargent at the ranch. *(Photo from Sargent family collection)*

foundation's endowment and proclaimed that he saw no reason for Phil and me, in Leonard's words, to "have all the fun after I am dead."

Leonard then added his personal accountant, Ernie Turner, to the board. Phil and I remained on the board while I also took on the duties of executive director. They were positions I held for the next 25 years. Every now and then there would be the suggestion that working full time for the state fish and wildlife agency while also serving as a board member and working part time as executive director for an environmental philanthropy created a "conflict of interest." My response always was that I preferred to see it as a "consistency of interest."

Since its inception, the Cinnabar Foundation adopted and remained focused on two important principles. The first was to limit the range of our philanthropy to Montana and the Greater Yellowstone Ecosystem. The second was to invite and consider grants for an organization's general operating expenses. Since Cinnabar's inception, dependable grassroots organizations have benefited from those basic principles. We also invited special project considerations to stimulate creativity while at the same time realizing the importance of day-to-day operations over the long term. By virtue of board member selection and distribution, the foundation remains close enough to the grassroots to observe and evaluate the effectiveness of the applicant organizations.

Although Cinnabar's first grants totaled only $1,123, as it passed it's quarter-century mark in 2008, Cinnabar was granting more than $400,000 per year to nearly 90 non-government conservation entities. When 2016 closed, the number of grants awarded since 1985 reached 1,790 in number and totaled $7.47 million. In addition, Cinnabar sponsored a variety of conferences and seminars to address conservation issues of the day and teach the depth of the conservation ethic in Montana and the Greater Yellowstone Ecosystem.

As all of this action and philanthropy was occurring, time also marched on. Acute myelogenous leukemia claimed Phil Tawney's life on January 9, 1995, long before we were prepared to lose him. Both Len and Sandy Sargent passed away in 1997. I cling to the hope that in the hereafter they now share, that their dunya, their physical place, is just like Cinnabar Basin—reserved for, and deserved by, them.

Shortly after Cinnabar passed its quarter-century mark, I let my term on the board of directors pass, thinking maybe I could be the first person to leave the Cinnabar Board alive. The rest of the board, however, changed the by-laws

Robin and Phil Tawney. Phil was a founding member of The Cinnabar
Foundation and Robin has chaired the Foundation Board since 1997.

and created a board-emeritus position and appointed me to
fill it. There have been a good number of precious, valued,
and deeply appreciated awards sent my way through the years,
but that action gave me more satisfaction than any of them.

A Couple More Laps
Around the Track

During the December 12, 1982, meeting with the governor, the director of MFWP, and Phil Tawney about closing the Ecological Services Division, it was frequently asserted that I would be retained and given "meaningful work." When the division's last budget expired on June 30, 1983, the division ceased to exist. After its personnel were assigned to other divisions, a three-person residual became the Resource Assessment Unit within the director's office. That occurred in July. All active field projects on the Front continued and strengthened the base of information to protect wildlife and other natural values.

In December 1984, the little Resource Assessment Unit got lucky. Sage Creek Coal Limited of Canada proposed a coal mine on Cabin and Howell Creeks in British Columbia. Both creeks were tributaries to the North Fork of the Flathead River. In addition to being a primary source of water for Flathead Lake, the North Fork is also the western boundary of Glacier National Park. No one south of the Canadian/U.S. border wanted to see an open-pit coal mine on that river. In addition, the MFWP had the equivalent of an environmental pit-bull on a short leash and muzzled in the basement. It looked like a match made in heaven.

Both the United States and Canada requested that the International Joint Commission examine and report on the mine's potential to possibly violate the Boundary Waters Treaty of 1909. Article IV of the treaty states that international

Jim and Gayle enjoying a day on the North Fork of the Flathead River.
(Photo by Stacy Kiser)

waters "shall not be polluted on either side to the injury or health or property on the other." In response, the U.S. and Canada established the Flathead River International Study Board to undertake a technical assessment as part of the commission's deliberations. The study board needed U.S. and Canadian co-chair persons, and I was assigned to represent the U.S. From my point of view, it certainly fit the definition of doing the promised "meaningful work." From the political side, there was no Montana politician willing to put the North Fork of the Flathead River, and the lake it ran into, at risk. Finally, at least for the duration of this assignment, the politicians and I were of one mind.

The technical assessment of the mine's potential to impact water quality took three and a half years and was done by a balanced team of scientists from the U.S. and Canada. In July 1988, we, the Flathead River International Study Board, issued our final report to the International Joint Commission. In December of that year, the International Joint Commission issued their findings and recommendations.

Their recommendations were:

> The Commission recommends that, in order that Governments can ensure that the provisions of Article IV of the Boundary Waters Treaty are honoured in the matter of the proposed coal mine at Cabin Creek in British Columbia:
>
> (1) the mine proposal as presently defined and understood not be approved;
>
> (2) The mine proposal not receive regulatory approval in the future unless and until it can be demonstrated that:
>
> (a) The potential transboundary impacts identified in the report of the Flathead International Study Board have been determined with reasonable certainty and would constitute a level of risk acceptable to both Governments; and
>
> (b) the potential impacts on the sport fish populations and habitat in the Flathead River system would not occur or could be fully mitigated in an effective and assured manner; and,
>
> (3) The Governments consider, with the appropriate jurisdictions, opportunities for defining and implementing compatible, equitable and sustainable development activities and management strategies in the upper Flathead River Basin.

During this four-year project we kept in close contact and communication with the citizens of the Flathead area, particularly those hearty souls who lived year-round up the North Fork of the Flathead River. One of those residents was John Frederick, who ran the general store in remote

Polebridge. Throughout this process, Rich Moy of the Montana Department of Natural Resources served as our U.S. secretary. When we received the news of the International Joint Commission's recommendations, Rich and I hatched a little plan. We decided to deliver the news to John personally.

A few days later, we were knocking on John's door when he, still in his bathrobe, answered. We gave him the news and handed him a copy of the Commission's decision. John went back into his house and returned with three small glasses. I poured a bit of brandy in each from a bottle brought for the occasion. We then toasted the river, the study team, the Commission, and the future of an exceptional wild place. It was a *golden moment* for the North Fork, and it was indeed "meaningful work." The North Fork of the Flathead was safe. In later years, Rich would be appointed to and serve as one of the U.S. Commissioners on the International Joint Commission. On November 15, 2017, John Frederick passed away. He left the North Fork of the Flathead River clean and strong. When his turn came, he took his best shot—and prevailed.

One More Lap in MFWP

As the issue of a coal mine on the upper North Fork of the Flathead River was nearing completion, I happened to be in Washington D. C. tending to some final details on the project and enjoying a modest thank-you-for-your-service ceremony. While in my hotel one morning I happened to be listening to a call-in radio program. It didn't take long to notice that virtually every caller wanted to talk about the shooting of Yellowstone buffalo. The ire and anger of the callers focused on the fact that every buffalo entering Montana was

Jim, John Frederick and Rich Moy toasting the North Fork decision. *(An early selfie)*

being shot; the number was escalating; and hunting was an evil activity.

It was the winter of 1988-1989, which came on the heels of some rather large forest/range fires in Yellowstone National Park during the summer of 1988. At the time, Montana had a state law requiring that every buffalo entering Montana from the park be killed because of the fear they might transmit brucellosis to domestic livestock. In prior years, the number killed had been modest, but fire and then snow pushed the buffalo carcass-count first toward 500 and then a bit beyond. Buffalo permits were issued by the state, and those who drew permits were often escorted to the buffalo by park rangers or game wardens. The anti-hunters and their organizations were having a field day, and we were giving them the national scandal they needed to stimulate their passion and fill their coffers.

While the Yellowstone-bison issue was running its course, Montana had a general election and chose Stan Stephens, a Republican, as governor to take office in January of 1989. He appointed K.L. Cool, a wildlife professional, to be the director of the Montana Department of Fish, Wildlife and Parks. The new director had a distinguished career with the South Dakota Department of Game, Fish and Parks and was a regional director for Ducks Unlimited when picked to head the Montana Department. He had no idea how I came to be attached to his office as a "special assistant." We both seemed content to just let it ride.

It may have been the new director's first staff meeting or close to it, and it involved all the department's seven regional supervisors and its five or so division administrators. The new director and his existing staff were still just getting acquainted. When an opportunity presented itself, I told the assembled of my recent experience listening to the call-in radio show in Washington D. C. All present were well aware of the bashing that hunting was taking over the legislatively mandated buffalo killing. When finished, I posed a question to the group: "Is there anyone in this room that thinks we are doing the right thing?" Not a hand was raised, the silence was absolute. The new director's jaw seemed to drop a bit as he quickly realized we had a problem.

The first step in resolving the problem was to repeal the law that required killing every buffalo leaving the park and entering Montana. With the support of the new governor and a courageous legislator or two, that was quickly accomplished. The legislative champion of repealing the old law was Bob Ream of Missoula. We also concluded that we had so damaged the image of hunting in America that we needed to find a way to atone for what we had been a party to. The idea we came up with was to host an international conference or symposium to engage in a critical self-examination of hunting. We proposed addressing what was right with hunting and where we may have gone wrong. This idea led to convening the first Governor's Symposium on North America's Hunting Heritage to address those very things.

The symposium idea caught on and quickly became international in scope. On July 16, Governor Stephens welcomed and challenged hunters from all across North America with these words:

> I hope that your discussions…lead to a renewed sense of purpose, perhaps even a renewed movement toward a collective conservation ethic, among all those who value wildlife, their habitats and the immeasurable quality they bring to our lives. It is time that we aired the hunting issue in full view of the American people.

Over the next three days a lot of words were spoken as the hunting community examined both its assets and its warts. In addition to a recognized need to "clean up our act" in regard to hunter behavior, the choices seemed to include both: "circle the wagons" and defend hunting based on our record; or, just continue to focus on wildlife restoration and conservation. Jay Hair of the National Wildlife Federation put it in the fewest words, saying, "The choice is clear, we either lead or become irrelevant."

There would be six more symposia held in the U.S. and Canada as part of this series. The series, for a time at least, focused both the government and private sector on hunting heritage and hunter ethics. As the series neared conclusion, a document titled "The North American Hunting Accord" was articulated and signed by sixty-three state, provincial, and private-sector wildlife conservation entities. The accord contained ten articles of agreement, including:

> Article 3: The North American hunting community will develop, articulate and personally adhere to ethical principles and practices, including the spirit of fair chase, which will guide their conduct before, during and after the hunt.

The years of conversation and articulation as the symposium series traveled through the U.S. and Canada clearly put the hunting community's focus on hunter behavior and hunting ethics. At the same time, it caused us all to learn more about the conservation heritage that produced us and that we now sought to revive in our defense of the hunt. While this turned out to be a good thing, it fell short of qualifying as a "golden moment."

On to Orion
and the Books

The first Governor's Symposium on the North American Hunting Heritage did conclude with a call to action. One speaker issued the following challenge:

> We must…"true" ourselves with our own heritage while we address an ethic that will fit the future. We must begin:
> • Managing habitat to provide ethical circumstances for fair chase rather than convenient circumstances for killing.
> • teaching a respect for the animals we pursue,
> • teaching an appreciation for the relationship between the animals and the earth we share,
> • encourage creation of coalitions built around hunters, anglers and other environmental interests,
> • defending the democracy of hunting and fishing in a world pressing to domesticate, privatize, and commercialize fish and wildlife.

In August 1993, about a year after this gauntlet was thrown down, I retired from the Montana Department of Fish, Wildlife and Parks and helped form Orion the Hunters Institute to pursue those purposes. I was partial to that particular challenge because it was the conclusion of the "Call to Action" paper I wrote and delivered at the symposium. If a person is not willing to follow their own advice,

Orion the Hunter's Institute logo

who will? Nine months later Phil Tawney filed the Articles of Incorporation creating Orion the Hunters Institute on March 17, 1994.

While all of this was going on, Bill Schneider, an old friend and publisher, tossed a small, somewhat worn little book into my lap. He asked me to write something like it about hunting ethics. I had never written a book before but the hunting community was focused on ethics at the time. Why not give it a try? With my career at Fish, Wildlife and Parks at the finish line, a part-time job as executive director of the Cinnabar Foundation supportive, and Orion the Hunters Institute ready to launch, it seemed like a sensible thing to do.

Beyond Fair Chase: The Ethic and Tradition of Hunting

The book tossed in my lap was Strunk and White's *The Elements of Style*. When endorsing Strunk and White's book, the *Boston Globe* observed: "No book in shorter space, with fewer words, will help any writer more than this persistent little volume." It was 92 pages and had been guiding writers since 1919. The local publisher then asked me to write something similar on hunting and hunter ethics. He wanted it simple, to the point, and brief.

When first asked to write the book, there was a lot of public attention directed at China's Communist Party Chairman Mao Tse Tung and his "Little Red Book" on communist ideology. It caused the publisher to suggest we call our effort on hunting and hunter ethics the "Little Brown Book." Feeling that we needed something a bit different, I eventually gave selected members of my local rod and gun club a draft of the text and invited them to have a few beers and talk over what we were trying to do. The main purpose, however, was to find a better title. There was a quick consensus that something better than "Little Brown Book" was needed. Before long Mike Trevor, a seasoned hunter, suggested *Beyond Fair Chase* and consensus was immediate.

In about six months a draft was in the hands of Falcon Press. The text was 112 pages but the small-sized paperback easily fit in a hunter's pocket. The next objective was to get it into the hands of the hunter education community. To that end Falcon printed a text only pre-publication edition of 3,000 copies to test the market. Copies of those books were given to the directors of the International Hunter Education Association (IHEA). The IHEA is an association of state and provincial hunter education coordinators and their volunteer grassroots hunter education instructors. The response from a number of those directors was quite favorable.

Encouraged by the news of a positive response, I contacted the Hunter Education Coordinator of Iowa where the next annual meeting of the IHEA was soon to be held. I told him my purpose was to tell the coordinators and instructors of the soon to be printed *Beyond Fair Chase*. I asked for any open space that might show up on their scheduled program, like a speaker or panelist canceling, just any time slot that might be or come open and that he needed to fill. He gave me the

"Awards Luncheon" speaker spot on the program.

The conference was held in the historic Hotel Fort Des Moines in May, 1994. I had carefully written a presentation that included a bit of Iowa conservation history. Thus, I was aware of the exceptional contributions of Jay Norwood (Ding) Darling, who launched his conservation career with the *Des Moines Register* as a writer and editorial cartoonist. It was a career that in time included being head of the Bureau of Biological Survey in Franklin D. Roosevelt's administration and a founder of the National Wildlife Federation. In addition, another native Iowan, Aldo Leopold, is still known as the father of wildlife management as well as the conservation movement's most profound philosopher. A presentation was crafted around some of the principles articulated and accomplishments realized by these giants.

Upon entering the Hotel Fort Des Moines' elegant old vintage dining area, with its dark polished hardwood décor, I simply assumed that this room had not changed since the hotel opened in 1919. That led to the assumption that this place was the center of Des Moines cultural activity through a period when the American conservation ethic was literally born, promoted, and advanced by some of its most articulate spokesmen. I was certain that "Ding" and "Aldo" had given speeches, lectures, and made presentations in that very same room. When it came time to speak, the prepared text was abandoned.

The talk presented, given extemporaneously, focused on the room and the words that had been spoken there. Words delivered by wildlife conservation giants. Words whose echoes remain buried within and held by the very walls that now surrounded and held us. This was spiced up with some direct

Leopold and Darling quotes remembered from the prepared text. It worked!

Chris Cauble of Falcon Press, and Gayle Joslin, working under contract with Falcon Press, had a table set up just outside the dining area. They were there to take pre-publication orders. When the luncheon ended they were swamped. Although the book in its final form with art work and illustrations had not yet been printed, more than 100,000 copies of the book were ordered. At least three states and one Canadian province ordered books for every student in their hunter education program that year. For our hunter ethics education commitment, it was indeed a golden moment in a very special room.

From the beginning, the book was designed to deliver a hunter ethics message through storytelling rather than lists of "thou shalt not" and "thou shall" do this or that. An exception was made when firearm safety was addressed. As Orion's years in hunter education unfolded, time taught us storytelling was by far the best approach to deliver a hunter ethics message that had the potential to stick in a person's mind. In the years that passed since *Beyond Fair Chase* was published, one story came back in one form or another more often than any of the other four stories blended into the book. It is an example of the effectiveness of storytelling as a teaching method. The story is golden.

My wife, Gayle Joslin, was the Helena-area wildlife biologist when *Beyond Fair Chase* was being written. One night she came home with the name and phone number of a hunter, Jim Gillespie, and told me I needed to talk to him. He had a story that I needed to capture. Jim had come to her office to discuss an elk season she was proposing for an area he hunted. In an extended conversation on elk and hunting, he told her the story of one of his recent hunts. Gayle thought it relevant to what I was working on.

When I called the hunter, he related how he had sent an arrow into a bull elk that he knew was a fatal shot. He watched the elk go down. While giving the elk a moment to expire, another bull elk sent a bugle over the countryside. The downed elk, perhaps getting a fresh shot of adrenalin, got back up and disappeared into the landscape. The hunter followed his tracks and blood spots until dark. He returned the next day, and the next, and every day for the next 30 days before he finally found the elk's scavenged remains and his fatal arrow. He then attached his elk license to the remains. Before long I had a draft of this story with the several significant ethical messages it carried.

As time passed, I sent the hunter my draft of the story, a draft of the book, a copy of the pre-publication version of the book, and the published book. In no case did he ever send a comment or even acknowledge receipt of the material. In subsequent years I traveled the country giving lectures and seminars on why and how to teach hunter ethics. In the process, hunters and hunter education instructors would tell me how the story of Jim Gillespie's "Wounded Bull" affected them and their students and the decisions they made while hunting. A good example was an Oregon hunter who wounded an elk. When darkness terminated his ability to keep tracking, he hiked back to the trailhead and retrieved a copy of *Beyond Fair Chase* from his pickup truck. He then hiked back to camp and by firelight read the story of the wounded bull to his hunting partners. On the spot they agreed, at first light, they would all search for the wounded elk. They were successful and found the elk in time to not only salvage the edible parts, but to fulfill their ethical responsibility to the elk, to themselves, and to each other.

More than a few years later, Gayle was running a big-game checking station north of Helena. One day while helping as a volunteer and fussing inside the station with some paperwork, she opened the door and said there was a hunter who just pulled in that I needed to meet. That someone was Mr. Gillespie. As I approached him he extended his hand. As we shook hands he smiled and said, "I'm your hunter." For me, that was indeed a golden moment. When asked why he never responded to the drafts and books sent his way, his response was simply, "Well, you got it right."

Other Books: The Hunting Heritage Theme

As the years at Orion the Hunters Institute passed, other books became part of the lifestyle of an educator. As those years unfolded from 1994 through 2012, three additional books were written and published. The second book, *Inherit The Hunt: A Journey into the Heart of American Hunting* was published in 1998. That book addressed how and why any individual in our American democracy can be a hunter. The story included a bit of personal history as an example of how the desire to hunt is simply a part of the human spirit. In the process of following the hunter's trail back through history, note was taken of some interesting individuals who forged a place for the common person as hunter in our New World democracy.

The third book, *Rifle in Hand: How Wild America was Saved*, grew out of our process of studying the American hunting heritage as we sought to be more effective teachers of that subject. Published in 2004, the book basically features Theodore Roosevelt's emergence as a conservationist. While

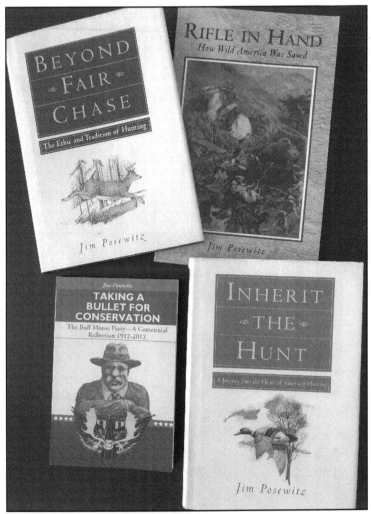

Books by Jim Posewitz

it documents many of TR's achievements, it also recognizes other significant contributors in a national perspective. There have been some genuine giants in the process of creating and sustaining the people's relationship to the wild in America. There has been a progression of individuals who literally changed the course of history. *Rifle in Hand* seeks to capture and help disseminate their stories. The hope is that it will stimulate writers and story tellers across this continent to do likewise before the stories get lost in the rotation of the many generations of North American hunters that it in fact produced.

Taking a Bullet for Conservation was the fourth book. It was written and self-published in 2012. The story is about Theodore Roosevelt's 1912 campaign to regain the presidency. As the 2012 general election approached, this little book was an effort to remind us that the current election was also the 100th anniversary of TR's effort to save the reforms he put in place as president from 1901 through 1908. The conservation component of those reforms was of monumental importance for wildlife, wild lands, and the American democracy of the wild we enjoy today. The book's title came from the fact that Roosevelt was shot during that campaign, and that whole story needs to be remembered in the context of what a committed person did for us hunters.

Orion The Hunters Institute and Hunter Education

The idea of a non-profit organization focused on hunter ethics and hunting heritage education was being discussed at the same time planning was under way to launch the inaugural Governor's Symposium on the North American Hunting Heritage. The first step in that direction was taken as a project of the Teller Wildlife Refuge. The refuge, located near Corvallis, Montana, was the project of Otto Teller from San Francisco, California. Otto was an exceptional conservationist who devoted a lifetime to preserving trout streams, organic agriculture, and the human environment. Phil Tawney, Brian Kahn, and I were on the Teller Board at the time and focused on the Orion idea.

Orion The Hunters Institute started as a project organized within the Teller group. An advisory board was assembled there in 1993. That board included: Ken Barrett of Bozeman as its chair; Dr. Ann Causey, professor at Auburn University, Alabama; Tim Crawford, conservationist and investor of Bozeman; Dr. Valerius Geist, wildlife professor at the University of Calgary, Alberta; Dr. Roy Jones, physician and surgeon, Lake Havasu City, Arizona; Gayle Joslin, wildlife biologist, Helena; Phil Tawney, attorney, Missoula; and myself, recently retired from Montana Fish, Wildlife and Parks.

In several trips, Gayle and I made to the Teller Refuge in the Bitterroot Valley, we often traveled with Phil. On one of those trips in September 1993, he fell asleep, which had never happened before. We made light of it, suggesting that perhaps my lecturing was indeed both redundant and boring. In October of that year, he called and gave us the news— it was acute myelogenous leukemia. On March 17, 1994, Phil Tawney filed the Articles of Incorporation creating Orion The Hunters Institute as an independent, stand-alone wildlife conservation and hunter advocacy organization. He brought Orion to life when he had less than ten months to live. Orion's 1995 annual report recognized Phil's passing. That recognition follows:

Thank You Phil Tawney

By Jim Posewitz

(From Orion's 1995 Annual Report)

In January of 1995 leukemia claimed the life of one of our founding board members. Phil will be missed, his mission will be sustained.

It was a typical September night in Montana' Bitterroot Valley, clear, cold and crisp. A board meeting of the Teller Wildlife Refuge had adjourned and Phil Tawney, former board member Brian Kahn, and I were spending the night. We sat around the stove, drank a bit of whiskey, and talked of hunting. Ever the visionary, Phil articulated the need to bring conservation history into the debate about hunting, to teach the more profound aspects of the hunting philosophy, and to address the ethical issues. It was the night Orion germinated.

When the vision crossed to reality, Phil was there on the founding board. We were one of many ideas that found substance under his guidance. Propelled by his exceptional energy and unrestrainable optimism Orion The Hunters Institute sprouted and now works to reach the full dimension of the dream we shared.

Phil was a hunter, as genuine as they come. He loved

and immersed himself in wild land, free rivers, and open spaces that flourished within him just as he lived within them. The following is from a letter Phil's sister shared:

"On Phil and (his brother) Jack's last elk hunting trip into Fish Creek... Phil expressed his true love for the outdoors. He was working late, so the rest of the party left a horse at the trailhead. Phil rode in by himself in the dark for eight miles with a bottle of Merlot. Those at the cabin heard him coming for miles, singing at the top of his lungs. The next morning, Phil and Jack watched three wolves running across an open ridge. Phil lectured Jack on how great Montana is - what a wonderful thing it is to live in a place where you can leave home and in a few hours see wolves in their natural habitat."

In June 1994, Phil and I talked of an October elk hunt and Fish Creek. We pretended the tubes feeding the chemotherapy into his body weren't part of the conversation. Before October the word "relapse" trashed our plan. In January 1995, the cancer took one of our leaders and we struggle to fill the hole in our dream.

Thank you Phil, for your song. It is the song of the wilderness, elk, wolves, swift antelope, and fat mallards. It is the song of the hunt and we shall sing it. Perhaps not as well as you, but sing it we shall, and pass it to hunters of tomorrow.

Laurie gigette McGrath

We had been incorporated as an independent organization for about three months when the entire staff of Orion The Hunters Institute took off for a conference on land and wildlife conservation on the opposite side of the planet. At the time I was the entire staff, and the effort took most of July 1994. Naturschutzbund of Germany was covering the costs; Orion was donating my time. The Orion board, however, was fully engaged in getting the organization ready for the road ahead on our side of the planet.

Starting Orion a Long Way From Home

It didn't take long for people interested in hunting to find Orion and utilize the hunting education aspiration we carried. One of the more interesting opportunities emerged shortly after our incorporation. It was an invitation to address "Hunting Economics" in Tscholpon-Ata. To get there you had to take a plane from New York City and fly east to Frankfurt, Germany. Then after a few days you take another flight eastward to Almaty, Kazakhzstan, where you then take a bus into neighboring Kyrghyzstan. The remaining travel from Bishkek, the capital of Kyrghyzstan, was either by bus or van, eventually arriving in Tscholpon-Ata.

There is a bit more to the story. This tale begins with the breakup of the Soviet Union in 1991. In the wake of that dramatic swing in governments of Eastern Europe and Central Asia, the Western European "Green Movement" focused on preventing an unrestrained exploitation of the emerging and vulnerable republics. For several generations these countries had been part of the Soviet Union. Among the leaders of this conservation movement was the German Nature Protection Society (*Naturshutzbund* or NABU). At the time of this trip, NABU had 300,000 members in Germany alone.

The European "Green Movement" had an intense interest in Native Americans, as did the people of Central Asia who see them as close relatives. In the course of time, I learned that NABU's invitation for my participation on this odyssey came through their connection with Montana's Blackfeet Tribe. The invitation came by telephone from Stephan Domke of Berlin, Germany. He wanted me to address the value of wildlife restoration and would cover my expenses. The itinerary called for a day or two with NABU in Frankfurt, a tour of Kyrghyzstan and their Tien-Shan Mountains, and a conference in Tscholpon-Ata. The objective was to encourage the new Kyrghyz government to favor protecting the Tien-Shan Mountains as part of the International Bioshperic Reserve Program under the United Nations. The mountains are the northern extension of the Tibetan Plateau. The offer was accepted.

The trip began on July 17, 1994, and ran through the end of that month. The 19th was spent in Germany with NABU and included a tour of a tomcat reintroduction project in the Spessart Forest. Lunch on that day was at the Gasthaus im Hochspessart, formerly a hunting lodge used by the bishops of that region. I had *wildschwine* (wild boar) *goulash* and like all German food it was delicious. That evening I presented a program on "Wilderness and the Badger Two Medicine" for NABU at the Frankfurt Zoo. My log for that day shows we then spent a few hours in a neighborhood *gasthaus* before returning to an apartment for the night. The trip-log notes: "Slept for ten hours."

Planning for the trip included negotiation for a ticket for Gayle to accompany me. However when they counseled us to bring our own drinking water and toilet paper, Gayle decided to pass. I packed both items. From Helena to Frankfurt the airlines indulged my baggage overweight without penalty. However, when boarding for Almaty, Lufthansa Airlines took note that my baggage was 15 kg overweight and they wanted an additional $600! In a last minute panic I repacked, leaving the water and tissue with my German hosts. This brought my luggage down to exactly the 20 kg allowed.

Once airborne, the navigation display noted we would fly over a small portion of Lithuania prior to turning south to Almaty. Thus, for a brief period, I was able to look down on the homeland my grandparents fled when Russian Czars were conscripting Lithuanian peasants for the Soviet-Sino War. I wondered who might have been in the seat I occupied had my grandfather let that happen. We landed in Almaty before dawn on July 21. From there we traveled by chartered bus to Bishkek, the capital of Kyrghyzstan. After meeting with Kyrgyhz officials we traveled to Tscholpon-Ata on Lake Issyk-Kul where the conference to discuss International Biospheric Reserve status for the Tien Shan Mountains was to be held and promoted. *"Issyk-Kul"* means "warm lake." Its surface area is more than 6,000 square kilometers, it is 668 meters deep, and slightly saline.

As we prepared for the conference, it became apparent that the text of my presentation needed simplification. The presentation format included a translator converting the spoken word from English into Russian and a second translator going from Russian to Kyrghyz. After the orientation regarding meeting details another vodka laden banquet was held, this time featuring fish from Lake Issyk-Kul. As the only North American present, my invitation to offer a toast was frequent. On this particular evening I toasted the clouds that hid the full moon that night: "I toast clouds tonight. They hide the moon thus it cannot see all the partying going on—

and report that to folks in Montana when it reaches the far side of the earth." We ended the evening skinny-dipping in Issyk-Kul.

The conference was held the next day and I sensed a bit of discomfort between my hosts and myself. My assignment was to describe the economic value of having robust wildlife populations. My experience with hunter-led North American wildlife restoration and conservation was an alien concept to the European conservationists. Their preference was to produce a resolution that precluded hunting. The primary hunt at that time was a government-run and guided hunt for Marco Polo (Argali) sheep. The government charged hunters, usually from the U.S or Japan, $35,000 for the privilege. At the time importing those trophies into the United States was banned by international endangered species agreement. It was a restriction that was, at the time, under challenge in U.S. Courts.

The whole dynamic of the trip suddenly changed with the Kyrghyz Minister of the Hunt and his team warming to my presence while the entourage I was traveling with cooled a bit. I sensed all this while being as far from home as a person could be without leaving the planet. The resolution being drafted contained the following: "Mass and hunting tourism must be excluded." I offered and drafted alternative language with some room for hunter-based conservation, and we discussed the issue for the next five days of touring the Tien Shan Mountains. On the final day, NABU settled on a slightly modified version stating: "Until a general concept for hunting of wild game will have been passed, hunting tourism must remain limited."

On the night of the conference, after the banquet and other social gatherings wound down, I was invited by the

Chief of Hunting to a private party in a rather dark hotel room. In the room were several men from the Ministry of the Hunt, a young woman serving snacks and vodka, and a person described as a "businessman." The businessman and the Chief of Hunting, both rather large men, were bare to the waist. After some discussion, all through translators, it became clear they were offering me money to take back to the U.S. to bribe the judge hearing the case challenging the ban on importing Marco Polo sheep trophies. I responded by telling them that it would be the worst possible thing to try and that I would not do it. A discussion ensued, most of it in Russian and Kyrghyz. At that point I noticed the female server had tears running down her face, and I suspected she was hearing things that no one was translating for me. At that point, I excused myself and left the room as quickly as possible.

Following the formal conference, the promised tour of the area was delivered—and it was delightful. It included meeting and camping with the nomadic grazers, watching superb horseman battle to get a beheaded goat across a goal line, and spending a week in the most open country I had ever been in. For the entire time we never saw a fence on the landscape or a contrail in the sky. Every morning and every evening we would scan the mountain slopes, the intermountain valleys, and the sweeping open foothills for wildlife. In all that time in this wildest of places, we never spotted a single game animal—none. At night while dining and visiting with the nomadic elders in their yurts, I would ask what wildlife was native to this place. They did not know.

Consistent with their tradition, we spent every evening in the nomadic grazers camps having a meal and informing the elders present of the mission to protect the Tien-Shan.

Jim searching for wildlife in Tien Shan mountains. *(Photo by Monika Zucht)*

These events always included vodka and toasting. On several occasions I offered the following toast: "I am from Montana U.S.A. It is a place of mountains, plains and a big open sky. I know many Native American Indians, and when I see your faces—I see their faces." As the toast worked its way through two translations there was always an audible and positive response. I would then conclude with something to the effect that, "I bring you their greetings and will return to them with yours." Their feeling of kinship with the Native Americans was quite strong.

On the last day we were offered a helicopter flight to spot some Marco Polo sheep in Kyrghyzstan's highest and incredibly rugged peaks, places simply not suitable for grazing domestic sheep and cattle. Until that time all the motor vehicles and machines we used were Russian items left behind when they pulled out. Mechanical breakdowns were frequent. While the Kyrghyz were competent and creative in making it all work, I decided not to risk a helicopter flight. The country's low ground is 3,000 feet in elevation and the high ground where the sheep were goes well beyond 15,000 feet. Finally, it was July and hot. All these things added up to—a bit too risky. Those who took the flight saw a few Marco Polo sheep and survived without incident. I chose to have tea and conversation with the U.S. Ambassador.

Four years later the Issyk-Kul Biosphere Reserve was established and included about 25 percent of the country's territory. This designation was recognized by UNESCO in 2001.

Not long after returning to the United States, I happened to be driving from New York City to Greenwich, Connecticut. On that short drive I saw more wildlife than I had seen in two weeks of travel with the nomadic grazers of the Tien Shan.

In a curious turn of events, thirteen years later a government delegation from Tajikistan visited Montana on a cultural exchange. While in Helena they expressed an interest in wildlife management. Their American hosts brought them to the Orion office where Gayle and I explained the North American Model of Wildlife Conservation. Tajikistan borders Kyrghyzstan on the south and a mountain pass that connects them (Pass Kyzyl Art) is over 14,000 feet above sea level. Their nearby Peak Lenin rises to over 23,000 feet. Montana's highest point, Granite Peak tops out at 12,807 feet above sea level. These Central Asian lands are indeed spectacular and awesome in their proportion. However, they all envy the wildlife abundance now restored to America through our democracy of the wild.

The Orion Message Closer to Home

Orion was originally organized as a project within the Teller Wildlife Refuge at Corvallis, Montana. A prospectus dated May 1992 described the effort in five words, "Dedicated to Sustaining the Hunt." A 1993 mission statement broadened the focus to include the animals and their environment, becoming "to sustain hunting and the resources essential to that purpose." Orion's first progress report was issued in January 1994. Among other things, it pledged to independently incorporate within the next three years. Three months later Phil Tawney had it done.

In addition to her taking leave from Montana Fish, Wildlife and Parks to launch the sale of *Beyond Fair Chase*, Gayle represented Orion as an instructor in an early "Becoming an Outdoor Woman" workshop. The event was held in Montana's Pioneer Mountains and attracted eighty women from 18 states. She then donated her instructor's honorarium to help Orion become operational.

We had been a stand-alone organization for less than a year when a young local hunter, Ralph Yaeger, volunteered his talent to the group. Ralph had a degree in business and experience in fund raising and technical writing. He told me he saw *Beyond Fair Chase* in a book store and read it right there before buying it and leaving the store. Instantly he became our development associate. Before too many years, Ralph earned us a major agreement with the U.S. Fish and Wildlife Service that put our education program into high gear. The grant covered our travel expenses, enabling us to offer the course free of charge to states while Orion covered the staff costs. By the time it expired in 1999, we had been in forty-one states holding seminars on "Why and How to Teach Hunter Ethics." We also carried our message to five

Canadian provinces using other funds to cover those costs. In the process, more than seventy such seminars were held and we reached somewhere in the vicinity of ten thousand instructors.

The Winsor Dinner

As the years with Orion ran their course we traveled throughout North America with the hunter's conservation legacy, always finding a way to cover the costs or donate the service. This was an activity shared by all members of the Orion team including an impressive list of board members who served over the years. Members likewise contributed. One such example was an idea Colorado hunter John Winsor laid at our doorstep. For us at Orion, it started with this letter from John:

> Something wonderful happened last Saturday night. Tish [John's wife] and I hosted a wild game dinner for about thirty friends. We asked other hunters to bring their game. We asked non-hunters to bring veggies, salads and desserts. We served Sockeye salmon (caught on Kodiak Island Alaska), bow-killed caribou (Quebec), elk and antelope (Wyoming), rifle killed venison (Colorado), wild turkey and quail (Kansas) and Pheasant (South Dakota)
> There were more than several anti-hunters who came to our party.
> I read the enclosed adaptation from your book *Beyond Fair Chase* before we sat down to dinner.

The following is John's adaptation:

> One of the primary purposes of hunting is to exercise our need remain a part of the natural world. We still have the desire to participate in the natural process.
>
> Our developed world is becoming separated from nature; it is becoming artificial. Our meat comes shrink-wrapped, supermarket stamped, with an expire date and price.... Even the outdoors is often delivered through the window of a tour bus, or processed through TV, videos and theme parks that mock reality.
>
> Hunting is one of the last ways we have to exercise our passion to belong to the earth, to be part of the natural world, to participate in the ecological drama, and to nuture the ember of wildness within ourselves.
>
> There is a lot to think about and be thankful for. It is well to think of these things when we claim an animal that is, in so many ways, a precious gift. It is a gift that comes to you from the ancestral hunters in the caves of our origins, from native hunters of all lands, from those who won our independence from kings, from our nation's first conservationists, and from those who work to protect wild places and the wildlife that lives there. Most of all it is a gift that comes from the land.
>
> Appreciate it!

John's letter went on to note: "Every anti-hunter took me aside or called the next day to tell me that for the first time, they better understood hunting." Before too long, Montana Governor Marc Racicot co-hosted Orion's first official "Winsor Dinner." Through the years, Orion has helped spread that idea all across North America in local rod and gun clubs and a variety of other venues.

Hunting goes to College

One of the more interesting projects that emerged with Orion the Hunters Institute was development and presentation of a graduate course on hunting at Montana State University. The for-credit course was developed in the history and philosophy department under the guidance of Gordon Brittan, PhD. It was titled: "The Ethics, History and Philosophy of the Hunt." Instructors included: Mary Zeiss Stange, Ph.D. (Skidmore College); Claude Evans, Ph.D. (Washington University); Thomas Baumeister, Ph. D. (Boone and Crockett Fellow); Deni Elliott, Ph.D. (University of Montana); and Bozeman, Montana, attorney James Goetz. Readings were also presented by writers Susan Ewing and Ted Kerasote, who were also Orion board members. The course was offered in the summer of 1998 and students taking the course for credit came from New York to California. The classes were open to the public and staff from the local wildlife agency and local conservation organizations attended.

Stepping Back from Orion

As Orion and its education programs traveled across North America, it was impossible not to cross the trail of Vermont game warden and educator Eric Nuse. In addition to his law enforcement resume, he was his home state's hunter education coordinator. Eric's participation in that activity in time led him to the position of Executive Vice President of the International Hunter Education Association. Eric also carried a deep knowledge of American conservation history, with key components of that history having played out in his home state of Vermont. It didn't take long to see we needed him on the Orion team. In 2006, Eric agreed and became a member of the Orion board of directors.

Spreading Orion's leadership from Montana to Vermont gave us all an improved perspective on the North American conservation ethic that was born in our wonderful democracy. For example, one of the seminal books in our conservation saga was written by George Perkins Marsh who was born in Woodstock, Vermont. The book, *Man and Nature*, was written in 1864 and is known today as the fountainhead of conservation. Gifford Pinchot called the book, "epoch making." Meanwhile, back in Montana, the first Territorial Legislature met that same year and passed a law restricting fishing to a hook and line. In many ways, it was an early if not the first expression of a conservation ethic in the American West.

It was instantly apparent that Eric and his supportive wife Ingrid were a perfect fit for Orion. On the personal level, I had been the executive director at Orion since its inception in 1994. Thus when Eric came aboard I was two years into my eighth decade and starting to experience a bit of wear and tear. Three years later, the board elected Eric president of the organization and asked him to be its new executive director. I was simultaneously honored by being asked to continue serving as a board member.

At this point in life I had amassed thirty-two years at Montana Department of Fish Wildlife and Parks, twenty-five years as founding board member and executive director at the Cinnabar Foundation, fifteen years as founding board member and executive director of Orion the Hunters Institute, and two years in the Third Infantry Division U.S. Army. At each stop, taking my best shot.

Still Bagging Trophies

Through many years wandering the rich Montana landscape, a broad and varied collection of more traditional trophies have been collected. When a lunker fish was caught, its image was often captured on film. Likewise, the same occurred after a day afield in pursuit of pheasant, mountain grouse, fat mallards, or now and then, Canadian geese. If an animal harvested had antler or horn, those were usually kept. Thus, after a half century, there is quite an accumulation of antler, a few head-mounts, and piles of photos. These trophies adorn our living space, our office space, our garages, a storage shed, and hang over the door of our sauna. To the best of my knowledge, not one of them has ever been "measured." They were and are trophy because they help take us back, back to the excitement in the anticipation, the challenge and intensity of the chase, the satisfaction in a clean and competent taking of an animal, the appreciation for what was given, and the effort invested in retrieval and processing what was given.

A Special Set of Antlers

My best example of a trophy is a modest set of antlers from a four-point mule deer taken by my first son, Eric. The antler set is a bit unusual in that in addition to the normal set of antlers, a short third independent spike emerged from the skull. The antlers remind me of the boy's excitement when he took the hunter education course and honed his shooting skills. Those antlers remind me of the day he took his first deer—a fine and tender mule deer doe—and how satisfied he was with that event. But most of all, they remind me of our last hunt together when he took that four-point buck. He had been off to college and other life adventures but was home for a hunt.

We chose a familiar place to hunt along the Continental Divide. It was a snowy morning and he worked his way along a timbered ridge while I trailed a short distance behind. Suddenly he stopped. His posture told me he was on to something. I likewise "froze" and watched the drama in front of me play out. It didn't take long and I don't think the deer knew what hit him. The kill was clean and instant. After dressing out the deer, we had quite a "drag" ahead of us. As we pulled that deer up one particularly steep slope, I remember telling him that when his youngest brother Andrew got to be of hunting age he had better be around because their "old man" would be worn-out by then. He promised he would, and we shared a laugh. Pulling that deer up that snowy slope with that young lad remains one of my biggest trophies.

A few years later, while studying math and foreign languages at the University of Montana, Eric died in a motorcycle crash. Those antlers, now on the wall of his brother's house, bring those memories back to mind. They are memories of the first son and how he brought the family into backpacking, and as a result, an appreciation for wilderness. They are memories of a free-spirited young man with a passion to ski who interrupted his college years to tour Europe and winter in their Alps. He was a determined young man and pretty good high school wrestler who helped finance his college years as an oil-field roughneck and boom-town bartender, all before he would see his 23rd birthday. Those antlers also serve to remind me of my own mortality and perhaps an opportunity to one day hunt for and find that son's spirit out among the stellar chaos of the cosmos.

Doug Ferris Story/Trophy

As my interest in the North American and Montana conservation ethic grew, I began to discover how unique our relationship with the wild has become in our American democracy. Even more amazing was the emergence of the wonderful people who brought this legacy to our time. When the 100th anniversary of Theodore Roosevelt's presidency approached, I suggested that a good Christmas gift would be anything written by or about Theodore Roosevelt (TR). My sons responded with vigor and I learned how much there was still to learn. After a trip to a used furniture store to buy a bookcase to hold it all, I got started.

As my mind wandered and searched the trails and tracks of conservation history, Joe, a 19th-century part-time hunting guide, showed up. In 1883, a twenty-four-year-old New York state legislator with a dream showed up in Little Missouri, North Dakota. He was there with the hope of killing a buffalo. In August of that year, North Dakota had their last commercial slaughter of buffalo. The New Yorker showed up in September, borrowed a gun big enough to kill a buffalo, and hired a local man, Joe Ferris, to help him find one. After a week of hunting, they finally found a lone bull wandering on Little Cannonball Creek, just inside the Montana Territory. The young hunter, Theodore Roosevelt, shot the buffalo and in his excitement of the moment did a war dance around the fallen bull.

About a century and a decade later, I was writing about TR's conservation legacy and working with Jim Stevens, a local illustrator and framing shop owner. Upon reading my text he told me that he had a customer who brought in memorabilia from the old Bull Moose Party convention of 1912 for framing. That was the year, and the political party, that backed TR's campaign to regain the presidency. I asked Jim what the person's name was and he said it was Doug Ferris. I went home and told Gayle we needed to find Doug Ferris. She immediately volunteered to find him because he had been her next-door neighbor for about ten years!

It didn't take her long to find Doug, who at that time, was living in an elder care home a few blocks from Montana's state capital. He immediately agreed to a visit, during which we learned that Doug was Joe Ferris' grandson!

It wasn't long before the year 2005 came along and we were preparing to celebrate the 100th year of the National Forest Service created during Roosevelt's presidency and TR's executive order putting the Elkhorn Mountains into the forest protection system. The Elkhorn Mountains are a wonderful wildland within sight of our state's capital city. To observe these two occasions, we worked with the Forest Service and prepared a celebration program to present in a local art theater, the Myrna Loy. Gayle brought Doug, now needing the assistance of a walker just to get around. She seated him front row center.

To kick off the evening's program, I asked Doug to stand up, and with Gayle's help he got to his feet in the isle in front of the first row. I then told the full-house audience the rather colorful story of "Theodore and Joe and that Last Buffalo." Then I introduced Helena resident Doug Ferris as the grandson of TR's guide. The assembled rose as one, giving the teary-eyed grandson of Joe a standing ovation.

While there is no way to hang that moment on a wall, it was indeed a trophy.

Five Hunters Pass in the Forest/Trophy

The battle over national forest and other public lands

recurs by the generation. In 1907, Congress tried to prevent Theodore Roosevelt from creating national forests in six western states. To our good fortune, he beat them and added sixteen million acres of forest reserves in those states. Following the 1910 fires in the Northern Rockies, politicians proposed selling all the impacted lands to private interests. TR and Gifford Pinchot beat them back and created some national forests in the eastern states as well. The "Sagebrush Rebellion" in the Reagan-Watt era had the same objective as did the armed terrorists that squatted on the wildlife refuge in Oregon early in the 21st Century. As hunters and anglers, we have been privileged to have a more sharing relationship with public lands and the restored wild resources they accommodate. My personal quest for the story of how public lands became so important to me, my family, and all Americans hit a high point in 2013 when I encountered three total strangers in a national forest.

A bit before dawn, I was sitting in a low saddle on the west side of a favored mountain in the Helena National Forest. My wife, Gayle, was going up the east side to hunt the high meadows. Just as dawn was breaking, what I took to be a father and two sons approached on the same trail I had walked in on. The father halted the two boys and they stood like poster students in a hunter education class—attentive, serious expressions, and guns under careful control. The father approached me and in a whisper said, "We don't want to get ahead of you."

As this event unfolded, Theodore Roosevelt's words rushed into my mind, comments he made on conserving forests and restoring wildlife for "generations within the womb of time." There we were, three of those generations, meeting in the public forest in pursuit of a restored wildlife resource. I responded to the father, "I think I know what I see here and I want you ahead of me." The father tells me the youngest boy has a permit to shoot a cow elk if one comes his way. I give the boy a thumbs-up sign and he lights up into a broad smile, his face absolutely glowing with excitement in the predawn.

Then words from TR's autobiography again rushed to mind, addressing why the public lands were protected by a host of his executive orders. He wrote:

> The things accomplished…were of immediate consequence to the economic well-being of our people. In addition, certain things were done of which the economic bearing was more remote, but which bore directly upon our welfare, because they add to the beauty of living and therefore to the joy of life.

As I watched the three hunters move on up the ridge, I realized I was observing generations now emerged from "the womb of time" to savor the "beauty of living" and taste "the joy of life." The emotion of the moment swelled out of control. I dropped my face into my hands and quietly wept. I have never taken a trophy that can, or ever will, match that moment.[29]

The M&M Bar in Butte, Montana

There is only one Butte, Montana, and its citizens frequently refer to their city as Butte, America. While there are many choices, the one saloon that most characterizes this place, and in a way the hard-nosed yet softhearted soul of

---

[29]Published in *Montana Wildlife*, a publication of the Montana Wildlife Federation. Vol. 39 #2 Spring 2016.

Montana, is the now historic M&M Bar. For years it was hard to do anything in Montana for any length of time without crossing its threshold. In the process of monitoring and treating some health issues, Gayle hauled me to Butte to see a specialist. The news was negative and we decided to have a beer before returning to Helena. It was four in the afternoon. We chose the M&M.

The place was empty except for the help and that included a young lady tending bar. She was a Missoula girl and nursing student at Montana Tech in Butte. In addition to a beer, Gayle and I decided to share a shot of Head Frame Whiskey, a local product. Typical of the place, a conversation soon sprouted with the usual saying hello and getting-acquainted talk. It was December, and at one point the sweet lady bartender made a huge mistake. Thinking in terms of ice and snow on this day, she asked, "How was the road from Helena?" Well the road from Helena to Butte is Interstate Highway 15, and in response she got the whole story of its construction and more. It included how a career was spent protecting streams, and how we tried to relocate the interstate highway through Whitehall instead of Butte to favor the Boulder River and Boulder River Canyon, how the Butte Rotary Club and politicians pummeled me at the time, and the answer probably included efforts to restore the Clark Fork River that starts just out the bar's front door and runs to Missoula where she was from, etc, etc. etc. The answer to her question then concluded with, "and that is why the road to Helena has all those tight curves and extra bridges!"

While all this was going on, this most pleasant and patient bartender asked questions and kept topping off our single-shot glass of Head Frame Whiskey. We did, however, have to navigate that crooked road back to Helena so we had to call it a day. I didn't know it at the moment, but I was on the cusp of bagging another wonderful trophy. As we got up to leave, I pushed some cash toward the young lady bartender to pay for the drinks. She smiled, shoved it back and said, "This one's on us."

The Last Mountain Goat

As the years piled on, taking their toll on the body, the passion to go afield to experience the *beauty of living* and the *joy of life* did not diminish. When it comes time to apply for the special permits to hunt moose, bighorn sheep, mountain goats, and antelope, I indulge my fantasies and apply for everything every year. The critters in the field try to counsel me. On a recent antelope hunt I found myself crossing a predawn landscape while favoring a worn-out knee joint and adjusting to a stiffening heart. While huffing, puffing, and shuffling across the gently sloped sage and grassland in the dark, I am almost certain I heard the antelope giggle! They were a generous lot however: later that day one offered itself and I gratefully and humbly accepted.

In the most recent special-permit drawing cycle, the Montana Department of Fish, Wildlife and Parks, to prove it was not without a sense of humor, offered me the right to purchase a mountain goat permit. Mountain goat hunting is indeed special. In 1957, about a month before responding to my military induction notice, I hunted and killed a mountain goat in the Crazy Mountains. Later, in the early 1970s, I drew a permit and harvested a beautiful mountain goat near the Gates of the Mountains Wilderness north of Helena.

The permit notification explained the option of not purchasing the permit and enabling the department to offer it to another hunter. To that person, I apologize. This particular

Jim–always happy in field or forest. *(Photo by Gayle Joslin)*

permit to take a mountain goat in the Mount Edith/Mount Baldy area of the Big Belt Mountains would not be filled. In younger days, my boys and I backpacked the area, visiting the high country and the lakes near the base of those mountains. I remember the place well, and if possible, I hope to walk in there one more time, maybe even see a goat. After many years of hunting, enjoying time afield, accepting the bounty nature provided, and savoring both the flesh and the memories of all that, the notion of celebrating it all, in this stage of my life, by killing one more mountain goat simply does not fit. The choice this hunter made in purchasing and holding the permit was to grant one special animal at least one additional year of life as a tiny way of saying thank you to all the wild things that so enriched this hunter's life.

It is certain that during the next annual cycle of that mountain goat's life, it shall welcome each sunrise looking out over a spectacular physical world. The goat's physical world, its

Mountain goat *(Photo by Jim Posewitz)*

dunya, is a beautiful place not changed much since Captains Lewis and Clark came up the Missouri River. It is a place that meets the needs and the preferences of mountain goats because the people with the power to destroy those necessities had the conservation ethic and the wisdom not to.

This hunter's *dunya* still includes the mountain home of this beautiful animal that is the color of winter. The hunter's imagination and fantasy will enable his mind to see what that mountain goat sees each glorious dawn and spectacular sunset. Because he has been to these places, there will be an appreciation for the rock crevasses that will shelter this exceptional animal during blizzards and raging winds. Likewise, there will be comfort in knowing there will be patches of lush green nourishment on scattered ledges and slopes come spring. The hunter's memories will perhaps temper his own reality rather than having it defined only by the walls around him and the ceiling above him. Having that unused mountain goat permit in hand will help make the fantasy a bit more credible. It will bring things full circle.

In Summary

Sixty-plus years in Montana has been quite a ride. As I became aware of the conservation ethic that emerged in the people and delivered exceptional outdoor amenities to my generation, the whole adventure was wonderfully enriched. Along the way, some valuable lessons were learned.

At the top of the list was the awareness of the unique relationship that is evolving between man and nature in our "New World Democracy." America's outdoor amenities belong to all of us. The right to their use and the responsibility for their welfare are all part of the deal.

Another valuable lesson from the perspective of a professional in the conservation field is to always cling to and be one with your constituent base. They are more important, more durable, and more reliable than passing political parades. In the end, it is the people who will preserve the democracy of the wild.

Also on the list of valuable lessons is that any one person, at any one time, can make a difference. Now it is your turn. *Take your best shot.*